MARKO POGAČNIK was born in 1944 in Kranj, and lives in Šempas, Slovenia. He worked in Conceptual Art and Land Art as a member of the OHO group during the years 1965–71. He has had exhibitions in Aktionsraum, Munich, the Museum of Modern Art, New York, and Venice Biennale. After 1979 he worked in the field of art combined with integral ecology (geomancy). He has developed a method of Earth healing called 'lithopuncture', which utilizes stones complemented with carved 'cosmograms'. His works stand in many countries around the world, including in Europe, South & North America, Africa and Asia. After 1998 he developed Gaia Touch body exercises to tune to the essence of the Earth and its transforming process. His books in English include: *Nature Spirits & Elemental Beings*, *Touching the Breath of Gaia*, *Turned Upside Down*, *Gaia's Quantum Leap*, *Sacred Geography* and *The Universe of the Human Body*. In 2016 he was appointed by the UNESCO Secretary General as Artist for Peace. Marko's website is www.markopogacnik.com

CHRIST POWER

AND EARTH WISDOM

SEARCHING FOR
THE FIFTH GOSPEL

Marko Pogačnik

CLAIRVIEW

Clairview Books Ltd.,
Russet, Sandy Lane,
West Hoathly,
W. Sussex RH19 4QQ

www.clairviewbooks.com

Published by Clairview Books 2019

First published in English by Findhorn Press, 1999

Originally published in German under the title *Erdsysteme und Christuskraft* by Droemer Knaur, 1998

Translated by Tony Mitton

© Marko Pogačnik 1997

A CIP catalogue record for this book is available from the British Library

ISBN 978 1 912992 10 2

Cover by Morgan Creative featuring image © Marko Pogačnik
Printed and bound by 4Edge Ltd, Essex

Contents

Foreword

by Tony Mitton (translator)

This book is different. It is packed with information which in itself is an experience, opening the reader to greater sensitivity and heightened perceptions. An ordinary book begins with a premise, develops arguments and leads to a conclusion, but in this work the reader will find that he or she is the main subject. Each chapter subliminally addresses different levels of heart and mind: the instinct for truth guiding intellect through the response of the heart; the sense of one's own long history out of past incarnations; the actual sense of the unity of the human race and our desire for love; the longing for real relationships with the human, natural and angelic worlds; the frustration as we confront the barriers which oppose us. And beyond all, the feeling of joy and awe which accompanies us as we recognize and surmount the obstacles, and go forward.

The book has many aspects. It tells stories; it researches and investigates; it travels to distant lands; in places it reeks of excitement, reading like a detective story as the author pursues his quest for the Fifth Gospel, which is the book's sub-title. He eventually discovers this woven into the Gospel texts in separate messages. These messages offer perspectives sharply different from the usual biblical interpretations. They speak of love and wholeness, male and female, and the union and communion of all humankind with Earth and the world of angelsv The dualism of good and evil has no part in them. Pogacnik concludes that the Fifth Gospel was edited out of the canonical texts, either because their message was too far removed from contemporary understanding, or because they interfered with plans for the formal, hierarchical theo-political structure which we know as the Church. Yet these messages are deeply meaningful for our present time and our transition to the next stage of our evolution.

Those who have been puzzled by the variations in the tone of the New Testament, which ranges from the widespread bestowal of blessings to unwarranted curses and damnation, will find here a key to determine which words were really spoken by Jesus and which have been interpolated. Pogacnik's method of distinguishing between true and false is carefully described and replicable. Authenticity is validated or disproved by the etheric structure of the text. The author brings a scientist's precision to his psychic abilities, and describes his methods exactly so that his conclusions are open to peer review by anyone gifted with psychic sense or able and willing to develop it.

The intellect is intrigued by these descriptions and the emotions engaged by the sheer drama of the quest. At the same time the plane of the soul is directly accessed from various angles: the reader participates as an observer in the miracle of transubstantiation; listens to intensely validating conversations with the elevated consciousnesses of elementals and angels; reads a moving account of the humanity of Jesus experienced in a previous lifetime; engages in an experience of the mystic union of Christ and Sophia, the Earth Goddess. And so comes to the incredible understanding that all these powers are part of us.

There is more here than the written word to work upon the soul. Pogacnik's inimitable sketches accompanying the text have a direct visual impact that reaches down within us, seeking the core from which they came. This is indeed the secret of the book, that it continues to work within long after the reading is finished, long after the reader may consciously have forgotten the words. If my own experience is any guide, insights and new approaches will occur, often in quite unrelated circumstances.

We are enjoined to love Earth for herself, not just for what she does for us. We are told that whatever we need for growth in any given moment is there for us, and so we should view every relationship and every event as meaningful for our wider understanding; and therefore to watch for the guidance from angelic realms which comes in impulses, happenings and new acquaintances, but to be discriminate. We need to become aware of the changes occurring now in Earth and in ourselves. And to understand that not one single person will be left behind when it is time for us to move forward to our next evolutionary step, which is to help make Earth the kingdom of God.

The book moves our consciousness forward so that we may become active participants in the evolutionary change rather than just passive observers. And indeed, active participants are urgently needed, for the usual contradiction obtains: on the one hand all is very, very well, and on the other we need to be actively engaged; on the eternal plane of the Spirit, the end is already accomplished, whereas on the plane of time we seem to be asleep and must wake up and be aware if we are not to linger on in a hell of our own making. Sure, there is always a Plan B, but no need to activate it yet again. And our failure to complete on time will seriously impede the evolution of Earth and of the angelic world with which humanity is linked.

The last chapter of the book places the responsibility squarely in our lap, not through intellectual exhortations and admonitions, but through a series of brief texts and commentaries provided for our further contemplation. This is our opportunity to discard fear, accept responsibility and work upon ourselves in wholeness and communion, which is the active spirit of this book.

Tony Mitton
April 7, 1999

*"Whoever believes that the All itself is deficient
is (himself) completely deficient."*

Words of Jesus
from the Gospel of Thomas, Log. 67.

Preface

Human evolution has now arrived at a decisive crossroads. The future of humankind on earth depends on whether people recognize their determining role in the evolution of the consciousness of Earth. To us has come the unique task of overcoming the thousand year old division between heaven and earth, spirit and matter. Heaven and earth desire to be united in the process of human evolution. At the beginning of our era, Jesus, who was later also called the Christ, pointed the way to Mankind's goal through his words and life. But in the following centuries his teaching became totally harnessed to the construction of a new world religion. Every single word of Jesus' teaching which his contemporaries preserved from forgetfulness has been given a role in the framework of the growing religious structure, a role which often diverges widely from the original intent. In this way, certainly, the words and deeds of Jesus have been successfully rescued from the silence of anonymity and brought into the consciousness of humankind, but their deeper message, which was intended for the climax presently occurring, has been lost in the process.

Now the time is ripe for recognition of the whole multilayered reality of the sayings and teachings of Jesus, and especially for the uncovering of that layer which relates to the evolution of humanity in the third millennium and which is important to us now, quite independently of the past.

The book in front of you concerns the discovery of a 'Fifth Gospel'. This was woven invisibly into the four named Gospels from their very beginnings, and its message is intended for the present time when great changes are taking place.

To its deciphering I have applied the different methods of investigation and perception which I have learned during my many years of working with earth-healing in the various dimensions of landscape and nature. These methods are described in the book to make quite clear the process I have used for dealing with the subject of my investigation.

This book represents my heartfelt attempt to work out a wide variety of ways in which to gain an insight into the holistic message of Christ, and in this way dismantle the obstacles which have arisen through the current extensive and outdated interpretations of Jesus' words in the four canonical gospels.

In my work I received help from many quarters. I wish especially to thank my daughter and co-worker Ana Pogacnik who received the messages from the angelic world for this book. Only a small portion of the messages received from the angel Michael on the theme of the 'Fifth Gospel' are here included. The most important part will be published independently. Also I must mention the collaboration of my editor Hanna Moog, which was devoted to more than smoothing the language of my German manuscript; I wish to thank her for insights into the fabric of the contents of the text, which made possible its refinement.

Finally, I should like to mention the drawings which I have put on paper— not only to offer additional information but above all to provide the reader with space which is sufficiently charged energetically to help him or her in their progress through the book. Some of these drawings are directly connected to the themes discussed in the text; others have a purely aesthetic character: drawings of sprouting twigs, flowers, pieces of dead wood, stones, crystals, and objects which have issued from a human hand. I have drawn them in such a way that they concentrate the powers of life, and so form a counterpart feeling-wise to the thought flow of the book.

Easter Sunday, April 12, 1998
Marko Pogacnik

Chapter 1

On the Quest of a Fifth Gospel

It was no accident that my first experience of that presence, which in Western culture we call the Christ, took place in Venice. Venice is one of the many places in Europe where the spiritual vision of Christianity has been embodied in a network of churches and monasteries; and this is amplified by a strong emotional quality for which Venice has its ever-present waters to thank. As is well-known, this unique city has been built in the middle of a sea-lagoon. The city's buildings soar directly from the water. This creates an ambiance where a heart encounter can occur which shakes a person to the very roots of their being.

The encounter came to pass by chance. On May 13, 1989, after a lengthy period of absence, I was visiting Venice to connect anew with my especially beloved little places, scattered throughout the whole city. And so towards evening I came into the Basilica of St. Mark's, its walls covered in golden mosaic, to experience once more the heart quality of its spaces. There I noticed that a little gate to the left of the altar, which formerly had always been closed, was now standing open. The notice, "Entry Prohibited," had been taken down, and I saw a few individuals hurrying to the gate and disappearing into the dark passage behind the door.

My interest was immediately awakened. I knew that the passage led into a narrow courtyard behind the church, and that this was only opened to the public on special occasions. For myself, I had not yet had the good fortune to be able to visit there. In the courtyard stood a Renaissance jewel, the chapel of St. Theodore, the work of Giorgio Spavanti around 1490. I guessed that the people whom I saw disappearing into the passageway were hurrying there to evening mass.

I seized the opportunity and followed them, although I did not plan to attend the mass. I felt drawn just to cast a quick glance into the celebrated chapel which, to my knowledge, must represent a supplementary pole to Saint Mark's Basilica. However, I did not succeed in merely satisfying my curiosity, for the service began the instant I stepped into the chapel. I remained standing by the door and decided that I would choose an appropriate moment to withdraw, using the time to visit other little places in the city. Then I noticed that, among the few, rather elderly people who had come to the mass, every eye was turned on me, a relatively younger man. A strange hope could be felt in their gaze, and I could not resist the pressure to seat myself and give myself over to the progress of the ritual.

Scarcely had I come to terms with the unexpected situation than I noticed an energy sphere pulsating high above the altar, directly beneath the vault of the apse. Its white light poured into the church's interior. I became firmly convinced that I was perceiving an angel of ceremonies who was accompanying the mass.

I was greatly surprised, for this was the first time that I saw with open eyes something that did not exist on the material plane. Admittedly, I had for long concerned myself with the invisible planes of reality and thus developed a special personal sensitivity. Up until now, this had expressed itself through a certain feeling in my hands which could "touch" into the subtle forces in my environment and distinguish them by their qualities. Now, how-ever, there was something new being added: a sort of inner looking that ran parallel to the perception of the physical eyes. On one plane, I could observe the actions of the officiating priest, an elderly man who obviously found his duties burdensome. At the same time, on the other plane I could perceive the calm rays of the white core of light which hovered above the altar. Then, at the moment that the priest made the sacrificial offering of bread and wine, an event occurred which left me dumbfounded. Vertically descending from above, a human-like figure manifested whose form was composed of fine threads of light. It was unmistakably recognizable as the figure of Christ which has been impressed on the common consciousness of our culture through countless works of art. Still later, as the Host was divided among the congregation flocking around the priest, I could perceive his presence in their midst. I even feel assured that I saw him lovingly touch some of the believers without their noticing. I felt pity for them in their stubbornness, and at the same time rejoiced that I was representing them.

It was not easy for me to fit this experience into my picture of the world. I have learned to pursue my spiritual path on my own, independent of any sort of institution or movement. Thanks to a personal discipline which I have built from my experiences, I have always sought a relationship with the inner core of my being and through it, like every other person, tried to come into resonance with the whole of creation. The relationship entails the cultivation of an inner silence and work on personal grounding. It is not a matter of following fixed forms, but rather a process which is to be perceived as constantly changing, so that it can be shaped differently every time.

After the experience in Venice, I had to admit that spiritual power, which until now I had thought to be free from forms of every sort, can also flow through an institutionalized framework which had seen no noteworthy change in centuries. This was an experience which gave me much to think on. In later, repeated observations of the Eucharist it remained true that it was impossible to deny the identity of Christ's presence which was changed into a human-like figure composed of a pure light-form and coupled with a special quality of feeling[1].

Through these experiences I became ever more convinced that these visions had meaning for my own evolutionary path. Finally, during my times of deep meditation, I began to concentrate on the figure of Christ as I had experienced it at the mass. It was on such an occasion, and with no expectations on my part, that this same figure emerged from the center of my heart and spoke to me. Admittedly I did not hear the words but I understood them in the following sense: in that period when his power and knowledge were incarnate and taught through Jesus, he made the promise of which the Gospels tell: Christ will be present with his blessing whenever bread is broken in his Name. It is this promise which is still kept today. What puzzled me, however, was the feeling of deep sorrow embedded in the statement.

As if to confirm my feeling, an intuition came to me which I would put into the following words: the purpose of Christ's original incarnation among men was to lead mankind into a new phase of evolution. This is the phase of independent spiritual evolution which can be accomplished not only by an influence deriving from outside, but also by reinforcement from within.

The Coming of Christ 'from without', such as I observed at the celebration of the mass, signifies only temporary support. People who admit the experience of his presence to their hearts, even quite unconsciously, experience an opening, an offer to join themselves to the Christ power within. The sorrow that I had felt stirring was because we all shy away from our potential, which is to take

1 See my description of a mass in the castle chapel at Turnich in *Die Landschaft der Gotttin*.

responsibility and independently incarnate what is aroused by the Christ impulse.

For me personally this insight resolved the conflict between the Coming of Christ 'from without' and his Coming 'from within'. It became clear that the Christ power can take either path to inspire or support people in their evolution. It is simply a matter of whether or not we are ready to proceed on our spiritual path independently. Whether the help comes from without or within is irrelevant.

For the next three years my attention was steered elsewhere. I had first seen the nature spirits, also called elemental beings, in the winter of 1993, or to put it more precisely, I did not see them with my physical eyes, but perceived them with my inner sight. Like the experience of the Christ presence described above, my perceptions in the elemental realm were also imbued with such a deeply gripping and inspiring feeling that I felt obliged to lay aside all reservations and uncertainties about their authenticity.

Up to that point in time, I had concerned myself almost exclusively with earth at the level of her forces, her vital energetic systems. It is their role to nourish the earth's surface, inclusive of all creatures dwelling there, and replenish it continuously with life forces of various sorts. For example, the 'vital energetic centers' or power points belong to these systems. These concentrate the life forces arising out of earth and then distribute them over the landscape. This distribution comes about partly through a fountain-like outpouring, and partly through the flow of power-pathways called ley-lines which carry and distribute the forces to the countryside. These ley-lines spread from the vital energetic center in question in the shape of a star and reach out across the landscape.

It would fill a whole book if I were to catalogue the individual force phenomena, so rich is the complexity of earth's systems[2]. Now the perception of the elemental beings

---

2 See my books *Schule der Geomantia* and *Wege der Erdheilung*, the latter published as *Healing the Heart of the Earth*, Findhorn Press 1998.

added a new dimension: the overall consciousness of Earth. My first unsystematic, almost casual observations of tree spirits, or of the elemental beings which enliven a river or dance through the air, soon solidified to a conviction that this was not a matter of individual beings inhabiting the earth, water, air or fire realms of the planet, but of an overall planetary consciousness. This consciousness concerns itself with the maintenance and further development of every little flower, every single beast or person, every mountain and every landscape on the surface of the earth. To carry out this almost unmanageable number of tasks, the overall consciousness of earth is individualized through a great variety of cells of consciousness, which we describe as elemental beings or nature spirits. In my experience, a fairy is not an individual being like a man or woman, but an individualized aspect of the overall consciousness of earth, one which takes care of a particular ambiance or space.

Over the years, the broader my insights into the multidimensionality of earth's systems, the clearer has become the key role that humanity plays in them. It is not only that we have diverted the greater part of earth's surface for our own needs and built over vast areas; not only that, through our practically uninterrupted battles and wars, we have put whole countries into a state of shock; we have also taken upon ourselves the right to grasp at the very being of life itself, and have pushed a specific level of existence — the material level — overwhelmingly into the foreground, so that others are shoveled into forgetfulness. By these others, I am thinking of the above-mentioned subtle levels. We have created a picture of the world that is distinguished by the exclusion of the overwhelming part of reality. This picture of the world does not just stay in our heads, but, because of our world-wide 'busyness', it oppresses quite shamelessly the life systems of earth. In brief, we believe that the earth is really as we see it in our one-dimensional view, and we misapprehend her true multi-dimensionality.

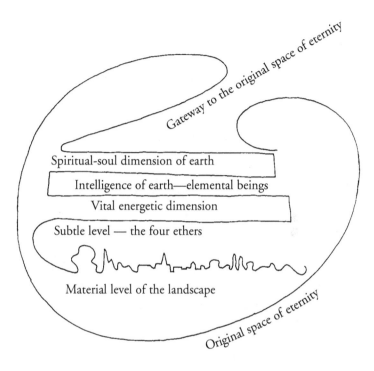

*One possible way of representing
the multi-dimensionality of the landscape.*

Anyone who has experienced earth's power, say in an earthquake or storm at sea, will have an inkling of the significance of such a perversion of earth's systems. There is only one way out of this crisis: a change in people's consciousness. We must change our basic attitudes towards ourselves and towards earth's systems. Then it will be relatively easy for Earth to 'dance' up and away from her present hampered performance. Of this I am convinced.

A consciousness change in humankind — yes! But what model should we follow? Who can move humankind to enter a process of change? We know very well that people are not inclined to leave the traveled path, especially when the changes envisaged are so far-reaching.

To answer these ever recurring questions, I was vouchsafed a vision which announced Christ's presence in another way. It happened during the night of April 17, 1996 after an evening presentation in Ottersburg, North Germany, while I was sleeping at a friend's house. Around three in the morning, I was suddenly awakened and made aware of a strange vibrational quality in the room. It took a little while before I adjusted to the unknown presence which was penetrating every atom of my being. Only then could I order my impressions and allow images to arise before my inner eye.

It was the same Christ presence, unmistakable after the experiences previously described. This time however, I did not sense it as being alone, but as inwardly connected with a second presence which felt as if twinned with that of Christ. I would however describe it as softer and womanly. I could best paraphrase the vision thus, that two spiritual beings were present in me and around me, and yet formed a single rounded whole.

I intuitively responded to this duality, and two names rose in my consciousness: Sophia and Christ. My mind wanted to interject that it would be more correct to recognize the pair as Mary the mother and her son Jesus.

The Blessed Virgin Mary shown with the Jesus child on the portal of the Lechkirche in Graz, Austria. The dragons symbolize the earth systems, and the crown the spiritual dimension. Mary, with the orb of wholeness, stands for Sophia; Jesus, who is gesturing towards the source of the Word, stands for Christ.

However, my feeling rejected this and gave me to understand that quite clearly it concerned one and the same presence, which, in a constantly changing rhythm, was showing two aspects of its being, one masculine and the other feminine. The mother-son relationship would bring in a certain distance which did not correspond to the unity which I perceived.

The vision continued to pulsate in and around me, and, using it as a mirror, I tried to understand as precisely as possible the meaning of these names which are so decisive for our culture. If Mary and Jesus stand for the names of two historical persons, then Sophia and Christ should stand for the two spiritual powers which have revealed themselves to humankind through the two persons. Translated as to their content, Sophia means 'The Wisdom of the Original Beginning' and Christ 'The Anointed of God'. Here we are dealing with symbolic names which indicate the feminine and masculine aspects of the Godhead, Goddess and God in one.

At the same moment, I noticed how these thoughts were diverting me from the direct experience of the divine presence; my mind was trying subliminally to control their effect on my consciousness. I took issue with the distraction and let go of the thought stream, opening myself feeling-wise to the sweet charm of the presence's vibration and letting its quality enter deep into my inner being.

After some while — I could not tell in terms of time how long the revelation lasted — I had the feeling that I was standing on the threshold of a new phase of my development; the touch of the Sophia-Christ Being sought to encourage me to take a step into the New, and at the same time indicate the nature of the task. Yet, just as it goes for most men these days, the inspiration was lost in daily chores over the following months. To be honest, it was as true for me as for many that I followed the common model of mankind and shied away from the changes which such a step would bring into my life. Later events also showed that I was not ready for them then.

Fortunately, during the summers of the last few years, I have been able to take at least 13 days off to pursue my further development. I withdraw with my family to a small, rocky island in the Adriatic, to meditate on my paths of personal development and sow the seeds for future activities. This time I would make my priority my relationship with the Christ power — securely based on the contact in Ottersburg.

On September 12, 1996, I was preparing a list of subjects to talk about in the following year when the theme of the 'Fifth Gospel' came into my head. Scarcely had I written the title down when additional explanatory words came to me, although I was not planning to provide commentaries for the different titles at that time. The explanation, which ran onto the paper as if of its own accord, stated: "There is no 'Fifth Gospel', taken by itself. Like an invisible network, it is woven into the four recognized Gospels. It speaks to that which men were incapable of understanding in the time of Jesus. For the first time, now, on the threshold of the third millennium, people are ready to hear it."

The message inspired my very depths. I wanted to leap into searching for the Fifth Gospel immediately, and then write a book about it. The following night I had a dream which I should have understood as warning me that I was not yet sufficiently mature for such a task. However, in my euphoria I was convinced that the dream was trying to warn me of disruptions emanating from certain contrary powers, which would try by their workings to dissuade me from the task I had just discovered. I regretted that I had not brought a Bible with me to the island, so as to start at once on unlocking the 'Fifth Gospel', in despite of all threatening dangers.

The Greek word for gospel, *euaggelion*, means 'health bringing message' and signifies the health bringing message

conveyed by the teaching and works of Jesus Christ in
Palestine at the beginning of our era. All the historically
established Christian institutions, whether they belong to
the Orthodox, Catholic or Protestant Churches, recognize
only four gospel texts as being faithful to the truth. These
were written by Matthew, Mark, Luke and John. These
four Gospels, established by decision of the early Church
Councils, became the basis on which Christian culture was
constructed in the centuries following.

Yet, from the time of its foundation, there has been a
suspicion within Christendom that the four Gospels —
they are called the canonical gospels — may not preserve
the whole of the Christian message. There may exist a 'Fifth
Gospel' which will impart all that was forgotten or excluded. The gospel fragments which have emerged here and
there since the Middle Ages can be counted as part of this
concept. They are called 'Apocrypha'. In Trieste during the
first half of the 19th-century Jakob Lorber wrote a 'Fifth
Gospel' which he called 'The Great Gospel of John'[3]. This
ran to about 20,000 manuscript pages, received through
the inner word. Rudolf Steiner published his spiritual sci-
entific investigation into the background of the life and
works of Christ under the title "The Fifth Gospel[4]." As a
seer, he could read the memories of that epoch — in the so-
called Akashic Record — and observe directly what the
writings had not preserved. In the years 1913-1914, he lec-
tured on the subject throughout Europe.

In 1945, the Gospel of Thomas was found at Nag
Hammadi in Egypt. This contains 114 of Jesus' sayings
translated into Coptic. This gospel was buried, along with
an array of Gnostic books, by a nearby monastic community; supposedly, this had happened in the sixth century

---

3 Jakob Lorber: *Das Grosse Evangelium Johannes.* 11 volumes. Verlag Zluhan,
  Bietigheim-Bissingen, Germany 1987. Condensed version, *The Great Gospel
  of John,* translated by Violet Ozols and published by Lorber Verlag,
  Bietigheim, Germany 1984.
4 Rudolf Steiner: *The Fifth Gospel.* Rudolf Steiner Press, London 1968.

The 'Jerusalem Cross'. Through the configuration
of the four crosses, symbolizing the four Gospels, a fifth
invisible cross is formed — a symbol for the fifth gospel.

and had been done to preserve the writings from threatened destruction by the official Church.

When I returned home from my island retreat, I rushed at once to the four gospels to look for the hidden references. I found none. The textual model of the gospels, excellent and logically constructed, presented no single tiny opening through which I could gaze into its interior. It seemed as if I was up against a brick wall. My intuitive trust, that within the textual structure of the four canonical gospels lay a 'Fifth Gospel', was severely tested.

When there seems no way out, I ask my daughter Ana Pogacnik for help. She has been communicating with angelic beings for the past seven years and we have worked together countless times on healing projects in town and country, in the course of which she has turned to the Angel of Earth Healing for the necessary information about the place where the work was to be carried out. This time I requested her to ask her angel teacher whether my intuition about a 'Fifth Gospel' made any sense. The reply, received on September 15, 1996, stated:

> *The four gospels are primarily devoted to people's relationship with each other, but the 'Fifth Gospel' speaks to the relationship which a single individual has with their own being, and to their relationship with their environment only as a consequence of that. It places the individual at the center point, as a person and not as part of a crowd. You can learn more about this matter from an angel who is 'active' in this area. He possesses insight into people's collective and individual evolution and helps one to search for one's personal spiritual path.*

> *The 'Fifth Gospel', in the sense that you have understood it, is an important source of inspiration for the evolution of humankind. It deals with a change in your evolutionary path, a great 'forward*

step' which is confronting humanity and all of creation. A whole host of angels is extremely active in this special area. They work by inspirational guidance, and by leading try to help. The angel I mentioned previously is one of them. His name is Michael.

It hardly needs saying that this message had a heady effect on my still rudimentary investigations. Certainly, the key had not been put directly in my hand, but the multidimensionality of the gospel texts had been confirmed. For the past 2000 years, the superficial, externally oriented dimension of the gospels had been the focus of attention. It had served as the basis for the construction of a religious institution which describes itself as the Christian Church. This had created a mediating authority which offered all people two things: the possibility of reuniting with the divine origin of their being through its priesthood; and of establishing a community resting on the commandment to love one's neighbor.

The other dimension, which I describe as the 'Fifth Gospel', is not perceptible when one reads the gospels in the usual way, because it lies, figuratively speaking, beneath the strata of external text. As characterized by the angel, its *content* is oriented quite differently. It does not put the commonality of mankind in the foreground, but instead gives priority to the individual. It contains instruction for the personal spiritual path which is shaped differently for every single man and woman, though that does not mean that a person should lose themselves in the labyrinth of their own personality. What the angel's message indicated was that new, deeply penetrating relationships with earth, nature and one's fellow humans would be made possible, grounded for the first time on the processes of personal self-knowledge.

The first messages which Ana received from the angel Michael in connection with the above very quickly formed a picture of what is meant by the personal spiritual path. In the first place, it does not mean what nowadays is canvassed about as New Age practice — there are no particular forms of meditation or prayer, no prescribed invocations or rituals and no esoteric disciplines. On the contrary, our quite normal, everyday life is presented as the most competent method of schooling the individual. The tasks and problems which our many-dimensioned life brings to every single person contain the opportunity for one's soul and spirit to ascend to perfection. It does not matter whether we recognize the divine plan in our life's path and give ourselves over to it, or whether we simply ignore it.

To give a small glimpse into this world of thought, I would like to quote from one of the earlier messages which Ana received from Michael on September 28, 1996, in Ljubljana, capital of Slovenia.

> *You are on different steps of your evolution, and that is the reason why you work together, completing one another. In evolution, no-one is more useful or more important than another, even though one person may stand on a higher evolutionary step. You are all essential to the general evolution and therefore to the Cosmos as a Whole. Everyone of you, man and woman, carries in yourselves a piece of the whole pattern, and also a message which has meaning for the onward path of all humanity. When you become capable of binding all these personal pieces and all your messages together into one whole, then only will you become a true community and be able to stride forward on your joyful way. No-one will be excluded from this unity, and no single person is unimportant in the Wholeness.*
>
> *In this, neither your age nor your profession has any importance. Only this is important, that you should learn to unfold the individual message which*

you carry within you, and apply it in your life. That means that you handle your personal life within the framework of collective evolution, so that it leads to the divine unity of all things.

One may have no trouble accepting the content of the message and yet still have doubts about its origin. Where is the world of angels? My intuition suggests that there is a richly articulated consciousness which pulsates between the divine dimension and the plane of manifested life — binding the innermost of the cosmos with its outermost. This is the realm of the angels. The name comes from the Greek word *angelos*, which means 'messenger'. Angels were perceived as messengers who travel between the sphere of the divine and the world of men. They are a personification of the cosmic consciousness. To better understand them in their being, we should release the image of their humanlike appearance and see them rather in the manner of a pure consciousness. Their 'body' is a vibrational structure which serves as the bearer of this consciousness.

For a person in the information age, such a concept should be easily comprehended. More difficult is the question of the various hierarchies of angels, as they were traditionally proposed. My hypothesis would view individual hierarchies as different outreach levels of the universal consciousness — that is to say of the angelic world. It must be understood that there is no distinction in eternity between consciousness and the beings who 'embody' this consciousness. The beings who are described as Seraphim and Cherubim can be understood as embodiments of specific qualities which pervade the whole universe and every single one of its parts: for example, the qualities of love, compassion or wisdom. The function of angels on the archangelic level is to infuse specific world developments or cultural revolutions with divine qualities. They were mentioned in the first quoted message as angels who support the evolution of mankind, inspiring and leading it. Among them is the angel named Michael. I will not call him 'archangel' because to do so would energize an outdated hierarchical model which in these times would act as an undesirable division between the two complementary worlds, the world of man and the realm of angelic consciousness.

Vastly encouraged by the messages from the realm of angels, I gave myself anew to the study of the four gospel texts. In so doing, I could take for granted that any help offered by the spiritual world would absolutely respect the independence of human evolution. Their messages never attempt to influence personal decisions — provided they are genuine. So it was with the search for the 'Fifth Gospel'. Certainly, I was strengthened in my intention and granted an insight into the nature of my objective, but I was given no direct indication how to reach my goal.

I began to re-read the gospel texts carefully, looking for possible entry points to lead me into their deeper layers. The reading process awakened many ideas and associations, but I could not say that I had found any real access to the pattern hidden in the gospel texts. Their perfectly composed external layers threw back all my attempts. After a month and a half's work, I was once again on the brink of despair.

On November 1, 1996, a dream came to my aid with a message. The dream began with a breakfast scene: I was busy with a small group of co-workers on a two-day landscape project. The first day's work was done and we were having breakfast on the morning of the second day. We were in the act of getting up from the table, and I was encouraging my co-workers to get to work immediately. Myself, I wanted to settle the bill for everyone's breakfast. I thought it could not cost more than 200-300 marks and I had that much on me. I was handed a bill for 5,000 marks. I thought I must be mad. This simply could not be!

In the second part of the dream, our fact-finding team continued walking through the countryside the whole long day, listing and mapping all the stones which had been placed there in Neolithic times. We found only simple standing stones, no exciting discoveries. In the evening, as we came tired and exhausted to the edge of the research area, I realized that I had left my jacket at our starting point. I was distressed. Now, I would have to go back the whole way on my own to get my jacket.

As I dragged myself unhappily back, I suddenly came upon a mighty megalithic monument which our investigation had overlooked. I could not understand how this had happened, considering the giant massiveness of this work of art. I remember exactly how it was composed of four pillars standing close together. Of particular interest to me were the pillars' capitals, which were fashioned in a manner characteristic of the Slovenian architect Josef Plecnik. It is true that I value his work immensely, but how could it be, I thought in my dream, that he had left behind traces of his creativity in the Neolithic age? Something inconceivable was becoming real. I could only stand amazed, and in this state of mind, I awoke.

I understood the last part of the dream immediately. It told me that there were certainly hidden 'treasures' in the four gospel texts, but that I was not capable of perceiving them. The first part of the dream would indicate why I was not capable. I succeeded in deciphering it after I made an association with the sixth chapter of Mark's gospel. This tells of the first of two occasions when Jesus fed a multitude. Jesus was teaching in a place far from human habitation, and 5,000 people had gathered around him. It was already becoming late and the disciples told Jesus of their concern that they had too little food to provide a meal for such a crowd. Jesus told them to count their provisions, and it turned out that they had only two fishes and five loaves of bread. Jesus had them distribute this sparse store among the 5,000 people, and amazingly, all were satisfied. After the meal they could even gather several baskets full of leftovers.

The numbers in the first part of my dream are conspicuously similar to those in the feeding of the people. In my dream, there were 200-300 marks at my disposal, and with these I was supposed to pay a bill of 5,000 marks. In the gospel account, there were two pieces of fish and five of bread, and these were supposed to satisfy 5,000 people. In both cases, there is no linear relationship between what is available and what is expected; instead a quantum leap is indicated, a logically unthinkable transference to a plane of higher potency.

In plain words, this told me that I was lingering on a plane of consciousness where I could expect no richly informative insights into the secrets of the 'Fifth Gospel'. I must undergo a process of inner change through which I would reach a higher plane of consciousness, indicated by the number five thousand. Only if I reached this plane, working on my personal development, would the information contained in the 'Fifth Gospel' become accessible.

The paradox was that the dream simultaneously offered me an insight of this sort. I had come to understand that certain events accompanying Jesus' teaching in Palestine were not concrete happenings but rather messages in an illustrated picture language which could reach people subliminally; if they were expressed in a direct manner, their multi-dimensional character would make them incomprehensible. In my understanding, one could view the feeding of the multitudes as such a message, transposed into picture language. It tells us that the teaching of Jesus was not about a linear continuation of the old religious teachings, but rather opening the road for humanity to a higher plane of consciousness, one which was not previously accessible.

This does not mean that one should think that all the events which the gospels tell of Jesus' three years of public work are mere metaphors. There is no doubt that there are among them stories which we can well comprehend to be Jesus' concrete acts. One example is the healing of a blind man in Bethsaida, about which Mark writes in the eighth chapter of his gospel (Mark 8:23-25). "He took the blind man by the hand and led him outside the village. Then, putting spittle on his eyes and laying his hands on him, he asked, 'Can you see anything?' The man who was beginning to see, replied, 'I can see people; they look like trees as they walk around.' Then he laid his hands on the man's eyes again and he saw clearly; he was cured, and he could see everything plainly and distinctly."

Here we see the accurate account of a two-phase healing process. In the first phase, the faculty of inner sight, that is to say 'sight' on the etheric plane, is given back to the blind man. He sees people as trees walking around, because on the etheric plane a person looks like a tree. His aura is similar to a tree's crown of leaves and man's etheric root system resembles the roots of a tree. The capacity to see on the material plane is reached only in the second phase of the healing process.

Chapter 2

Testing the Etheric Layers of the Gospel Texts

Ether can best be understood as the subtle substance which provides the building blocks of the vital energetic plane of reality. Just as matter is the building material of the concrete, manifested plane of our world, so ether is the building material of the plane of subtle power. The western understanding of ether corresponds to chi'i among the Chinese and to prana in India. However, hidden behind this bare definition is a whole palette of varied etheric phenomena. Some of these relate to the subtle planes of the landscape, others to the subtle body of living beings, and yet others to the force fields which surround and penetrate objects. Because we are here interested in the etheric layers of the gospel texts, we should look at the last-named group more closely.

In my experience, every object displays an etheric form beside the physical. In fact, they do not so much stand beside each other, but mutually interpenetrate. The etheric form is often broader than its physical complement, but in some cases it is thinner. When broader, it is perceived as an aura surrounding the corresponding phenomenon; when thinner, it appears as a delicate shape which vibrates within the object under investigation. Just as one can see the physical form of an object with one's bodily eyes, so it is possible, on a more subtle level of perception, to sense the corresponding etheric form and scan it with one's feelings.

It is surprising how much is expressed by an object's etheric form which is not ascertainable from the physical. Such expressions usually pertain to traces of emotion, or qualities of thought or feeling. For example, if a bowl has been used over an extensive period for stirring some liquid, this motion can be 'seen' in the etheric form, even though the bowl has not been used for a long time. To keep to this example, if the bowl has served a ritual function, then its etheric form will be enriched by a specific quality.

A text is also a sort of object. The letters represent its physical form; they are supplemented by a sort of 'standing wave'. This is the etheric stream accompanying the text. To put it more precisely, the physical line where the letters stand in a row next to each other is woven about with an etheric layer. This etheric layer resembles an ordinary woven pattern and it contains information. For example, the way the pattern is formed enables one to read the motives which led the author to write the related text. Furthermore, the strength of the etheric wave testifies to the power of the inspirational source behind the written text. The etheric stream accompanying a newspaper article is as thin and attenuated as a thread of silk; on the other hand, if a text was inspired by divine power, it is strongly impressed and stands high above the lines of physical text.

I must emphasize that both the planes of text, the etheric and the physical, are relatively independent of each other. The etheric form is not affected by the frequency and manner in which the physical text has been duplicated. Also, multiple translations from one language to another change it hardly at all. Even the quality of translation can do little to alter the etheric body of a text.

On the other hand, an alteration of its content does affect the etheric body of a text, leaving behind it a clear track which indicates that an alien power has flowed into its organism. The quality of the etheric body changes drastically at the place of such an intrusion and is to be sensed quite differently. A few years before, when I was preparing a lecture on the Passion according to John, I had found some such examples in his Gospel.

There is no doubt that the text of John's Gospel derives from very high inspiration. Its etheric body is extraordinarily subtle and strong, making a structure that surrounds each line like a layer of cloud several centimeters thick. This causes the foreign parts of the text — which are scarcely noticeable otherwise — to feel so much more unpleasant to the subtle sense. For example, the beginning of the 13th chapter describes the preparations for Jesus' last supper with his disciples. There comes the moment when Jesus rises from the table, pours water into a bowl and begins to wash his disciples' feet. He tells them: "If I, then, the Lord and Master, have washed your feet, you must wash each other's feet. I have given you an example so that you may copy what I have done to you." The etheric body of the text is high and strong up to the very point that these words were spoken. Then comes a fearful crash to level zero. The etheric body now looks quite wasted away, as much in its quantity as in its quality. What is written there? After the words quoted above, Jesus purports to say, "In all truth I tell you, no servant is greater than his master, no messenger is greater than the one who sent him. Now that you know this, blessed are you if you behave accordingly." These are the words which carry the alien etheric body. Afterwards, as the text proceeds, the etheric layer rebuilds itself. Let us examine how it came to crash.

In the first part of the gospel message quoted above, Jesus' words and actions introduce a non-hierarchical order among the apostles; and here, the apostles are to be understood as representative of humankind. If the master, meaning a person standing on the highest level of the hierarchy, washes his pupils' feet, which is the lowest part of their body, the hierarchical order is turned upside down. In place of a static power pyramid, we have a cyclical grouping which joins the highest in a circle with the lowest. Or, as Jesus puts it elsewhere, "Anyone who wants to become great among you must be your servant..." (Mat 20:26).

Contradicting this statement, the second part of the text puts the old hierarchical model firmly back in power. This is a complete reversal, which is only the more reinforced by the moral imperative formulated in the final sentence. Power-hungry despots have forever insisted on just such a statement: the lord is the head of society and all others have to obey him.

Did Jesus come to strengthen the old order which oppressed his fellow men? The gospels say he expressly distanced himself from such a stance. It is conceivable however that, at the time when the texts were consolidated, the second part was added at the instance of some power elite who wanted to safeguard their continued existence with words issuing from the mouth of Jesus. But why should we concern ourselves today with power struggles which took place in the first centuries of our era?

Over the last two years, I have been able to refine my capacity to perceive etheric phenomena. It has developed to the point that I can now distinguish between the different types of ether which are traditionally classified according to the original model of the four elements — earth, water, air and fire.

To briefly describe their functions, the layer of earth ether lies closest to the physical form and its presence gives the relevant object its basic structure. Water ether may also be descriptively called life ether, for it represents the living breath which gives life to the forms. Or in other cases, water ether can serve as a store of the various feeling qualities. Air ether is the bearer of the consciousness function in space, i.e., outside the physical form; it serves as a storehouse of memories and makes possible avenues of communication. Fire ether can best be understood as mediating

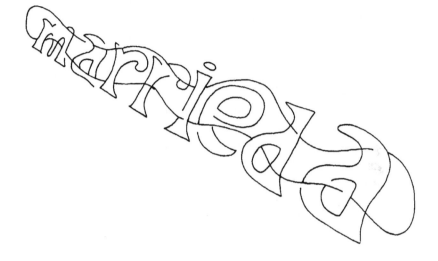

*Letters of a gospel text which is true to the words of Jesus
interwoven with the earth ether.*

spiritual impulses and influences on the plane of power.

The discovery that there are resonance points on the human body which correspond to the qualities of each of the four elements enabled me to work out a perceptual method of distinguishing between the four etheric forms. I use my right hand to activate the corresponding point on my own body, and can then contact the related etheric layer with my left.

When I use this method to touch into the etheric web of the gospel texts, they present a more or less unified pattern, only differentiated according to their four etheric layers. However, this is true only for those statements on which one can count as truly reporting the tradition of Jesus' words, with every doubt excluded.

If this is the case, the earth ether runs along the lines, leaning close against the text. It feels as if it is woven within the rows of letters. Above it flows a layer of water ether. Fire ether is especially striking when the text has come into being through divine inspiration. To the inner sight, it appears as if a little 'stave' of pure gold is erected vertically over every letter, its height varying between three and five centimeters. One's fingers can quite easily feel this fiery ridge, rising high above the lines of text. The air ether lies somewhat higher still, like a layer of cloud.

Armed with this new knowledge, I could examine with greater precision what happens when in the reading of a gospel text, I come upon a part which is alien to it. What I described above as a collapse in the quality of the ether relates to the layer of fire ether. This disappears the moment that the lofty inspiration which accompanies the works and teaching of Jesus is no longer present. It feels as if the fire ether has flowed away into the material of the book.

In such a case, the earth ether shows a contrary tendency. It detaches itself from the line of letters and begins to 'swim' over the text. One can interpret this as signifying that the statements are no longer grounded and,

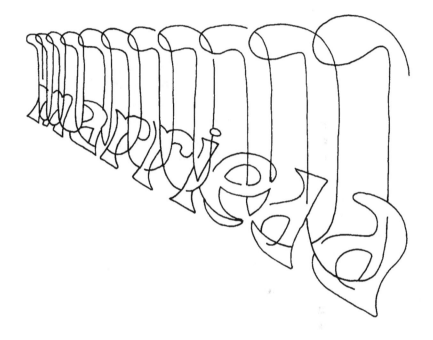

*The same fragment of gospel text showing
the 'staves' of fire ether.*

instead of being life-related, are laden with troublesome, head-related ideas. The change is not so marked in the case of the other two ether layers — water and air. I believe that this is because there is a plane of overall, organizing logic embracing the whole body of the four gospels and the alien intrusions in the text still belong to this. I will expand further on this point at the end of the chapter.

As the first subject of my investigation I chose a well-known parable which is found in Luke and Matthew. It concerns a man who arranged a great feast and invited many guests. "When the time for the banquet came, he sent his servant to say to those who had been invited, 'Come along: everything is ready now.' But all alike started to make excuses." One had to see to a piece of land which he had just bought. Another had bought a span of five oxen and was on his way to try them out, and so on.

"Then the householder, in a rage, said to his servant, 'Go out quickly into the streets and alleys of the town and bring in here the poor, the crippled, the blind and the lame... to make sure my house is full." (Luke 14: 21-24).

The parable is completely validated by the four etheric layers. The robustness of the fire ether stands high above the lines of text, and trail of the earth ether is woven close among them. Both witness that we are dealing here with a message that faithfully reports the words of Jesus. Transposed from the picture language of the parable, the meaning, to my mind, is that first things come first. When the deepest source, welling up from within, invites a person to turn towards it, they should let go of everything that can hinder them and devote themselves to it fully. To put it another way, a person should put aside even the most apparently important business once the time has matured to reconnect with the divine foundation of their being. The more that people, through their place in society, have lost their 'road-holding sense', the harder it will be for them to devote themselves to what is essential.

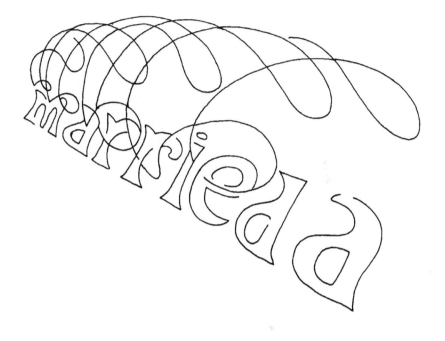

*The same fragment of gospel text showing
the layer of the air ether.*

This is why Jesus says that those who are not burdened with ties of a social sort have higher rank on the road to self-knowledge. They are symbolized by the poor, crippled, blind and lame. One can find parallels in other of his sayings, for instance, " I bless you, Father... for hiding these things from the learned and the clever and revealing them to little children." (Mat 11:25).

Agreeing overall with this message, Luke's gospel ends the parable of the lord's feast with the simple words, "Because, I tell you, not one of those who were invited shall have a taste of my banquet." The parable is also confirmed in this same form by the above-mentioned discoveries at Nag Hammadi. In Matthew, on the other hand, the text is modified. Now the story tells of a royal wedding feast which a king has ordered in honor of his son. Instead of the 'poor, crippled, blind and lame', those now brought in from the street are described as 'both bad and good'. And at the close of Matthew's version of the parable a whole new section is added. Here it is told that when the king is looking at the guests brought in from the street, he notices a man who is without wedding garments. When asked how he could appear without a robe fit for a festival, the man can give no answer. "Then the king said to the attendants, 'Bind him hand and foot and throw him into the darkness outside, where there will be weeping and grinding of teeth." (Mat 22:13).

The etheric body presented by this last section is completely alien. The fire ether, bearer of divine inspiration, has disappeared. The earth ether hovers in the air, detached from the lines of text. The layer of water ether, bearer of the life impulse, has become quite weak and 'dirty'. When I absorb myself in the information which I describe as 'dirt', I uncover an emotional quality of fear which is interwoven with a powerful portion of guilt. These are certainly not the vibrational qualities in which people should be sharing when they read a message from Christ!

I trace these negative qualities to the profound insecurity which this addition to the parable arouses in the reader. We are here presented with a power which can condemn a person to eternal damnation against all reasons of healthy commonsense. Someone who, without notice, is invited off the street to a royal feast cannot be expected to be wearing festival clothing. If one believes the added portion of text, he can be mercilessly condemned despite his obvious innocence. This creates a sense of total insecurity which must make everyone afraid.

One asks, how did such alien bodies arrive in the gospel texts? There is one answer in terms of form and another in terms of content. In terms of form, we should realize that the words of Christ's, as we know them today, were not written down during his lifetime. Some decades passed before the first gospels were authored and during this time they were transmitted by word of mouth. One can further project that the first gospel texts were not set down with the intention of capturing the events faithfully and truthfully, but with the goal of winning people to the Christian faith, or of gaining credibility for a particular orientation within the rich diversity of the Christian movement. In the end, the final version of the four gospels was decided by the Church Councils. One can imagine the radical changes which Christ's message must have undergone as it passed through all these phases. And this does not even address the problem of accurate translation.

In terms of content, Jesus himself provides the answer to the question in his parable of the tares[1]. The parable concerns "A man who sowed good seed in his field. While everybody was asleep his enemy came, sowed darnel all

---

1 (Translator's note. In what follows, the words 'tares' and 'darnel' should be regarded as interchangeable. According to Webster's Dictionary, 'tares' are a species of wild vetch, supposed to be the darnel, and this is the word used in The New Jerusalem Bible, which is the translation adopted here for all biblical quotations unless otherwise stated. However, the title 'parable of the tares' has been continued because this is how the parable is familiarly known).

among the wheat, and made off. When the new wheat sprouted and ripened, then the darnel appeared as well. The owner's laborers went to him and said, 'Sir, was it not good seed that you sowed in your field? If so, where does the darnel come from?' He said to them, 'Some enemy has done this.' And the laborers said, 'Do you want us to go and weed it out?' But he said, 'No, because when you weed out the darnel you might pull up the wheat with it. Let them both grow till the harvest.'" (Mat 13:24).

In this parable, Jesus confirms that both difficult and joyful experiences belong to the basic pattern of our life's path. One cannot say that the one is good and the other bad, for we must experience both aspects for our inner growth. Only when a person knows the shadow side can they consciously treasure the one filled with light. It is because of this that the parable closes with the words, "And at harvest time I shall say to the reapers: 'First collect the darnel and tie it in bundles to be burnt, then gather the wheat into my barn.'" (Mat 13:30).

In plain speech this means that sooner or later as they proceed on their path, people mature to the point that they can distinguish the constructive from the destructive. Then they can base their future development upon the constructive experiences, and take what they have learned from the painful ones. These last are then released in an act of forgiveness, in other words, burnt away.

One should know that darnel is a species of wild vetch. This description is confirmed by the discoveries at Nag Hammadi (Tm, Log. 57)[2]. The wild vetch is a plant which develops such thick stems that in Palestine it was dried and used as kindling. This emphasizes once again that the burn-

---

2 The discoveries at Nag Hammadi include a manuscript of the Gospel of Thomas. This is not composed of verses like the four canonical gospels, but of Jesus' individual sayings which are indicated as 'Logion'. They are quoted here and elsewhere with the abbreviation "Tm, Log....".

ing of the darnel is not meant to be an act of damnation. Quite the opposite, the apparently vicious is raised to usefulness.

The author of the gospel named after the apostle Matthew has added some verses a little further on which give an entirely different meaning to the parable of the tares. The etheric layers of this interpretation, purportedly coming from the mouth of Jesus, display none of the marks of truth. It is an alien body within the gospel message and not divinely inspired. These verses turn the burning of the darnel into an act of damnation, although the burning was appropriate to its traditional use as kindling, a use with which Jesus as a man of the people would have been familiar. "The Son of man will send his angels and they will gather out of his kingdom all causes of falling and all who do evil, and throw them into the blazing furnace, where there will be weeping and grinding of teeth." (Mat 13:41). Unhappily, during the past two millennia we people of the western lands have too often followed the false interpretation of the parable of the tares. Too often we have equipped and sent out armies which have fallen mercilessly on their fellow men because we have supposed that they were 'false', worshipped false gods or interpreted the tradition of Christ's message differently. We have tried to exterminate them as 'tares'. And is this not still going on today in my own neighborhood under the pretext of 'ethnic cleansing'?

In view of these misunderstandings, still being practiced, we must ask what should be our attitude to the realization that the interpretation of the parable in Matthew has led men into tragic error. Should we follow the same pattern, and accuse and pour shame on the Church Fathers because they were so careless and unaware as to proclaim such alien parts of the gospels as the Word of God, and require the faithful to follow them unconditionally? No, it would be not only senseless but ethically untenable to follow a pattern which we can recognize as already outdated.

Instead of that, let us take to heart and reflect on the original teaching which Jesus presented in the parable of the tares. The moment which one takes for reflection is a unique opportunity to decide on a completely new path for oneself. Let us learn for the future from our collective mistakes of the past. I say 'collective mistakes' deliberately, for they were committed not only by those who secretly smuggled such alien portions into the gospel texts, but by those who, by an exaggerated abandon to the words of Jesus, did not think and decide independently for themselves. These last have failed too because they have overlooked the fine distinction between what is true and what diverges from the truth. Today, we can all grow inwardly as we learn from the many-sided mistakes committed in the past. If, beyond that, the Church and society could decide as a whole to acknowledge their mistakes, then the troubled relationships in our world would in great part be settled and clarified.

Chapter 3

The Invisible Archetypal Pattern of the Gospels

The investigation into the etheric layers of the gospel texts had started very promisingly, but had resulted in no direct insights into the coveted 'Fifth Gospel'. Rather, I had been able to learn only where the object of my search was not to be found. The method I was using is supremely suited to define the differences between the original messages of Christ and the accretions originating in an alien thought-form. However, it is too coarse a tool to decipher the different dimensions of the message itself. To put it another way, the method can certainly confirm that the desired message is available within a certain section of text; but to bring it to light, another instrument would be needed.

One avenue to investigate was the plane concerned with the overall organization of etheric phenomena, which I call the 'archetypal plane'. I know of it through my work deciphering the force-systems of places and landscapes. This plane is concerned with the archetypal patterns which guide the life forces on the earth's surface. Based on the type of pattern, these etheric forces are not only guided but defined as to their respective quality. To put it more clearly, what we perceive as the special character of a place is established and maintained by the archetypal pattern vibrating in the background. *Vice-versa*, one can say that it is by a person's recognizing a place's archetypal pattern that its innermost being is revealed to him or her.

At the same time, the archetypal pattern presents us with a universal language for communication between all the worlds, planes, presences and beings which are woven into the life processes of our cosmos. This language has a picture-like character and is composed of single signs based on the archetypal patterns. I call these cosmograms. One could say that cosmograms are the archetypal patterns transposed into form. It is unimportant whether these are geometric, symbolic or anthropomorphic forms. To be effective as cosmograms, they must stand in an unambiguous relationship to their relevant archetype. Just as important is that their originating impulse should be of such high inspiration that it offers a communications channel wide enough to be used by presences from the non-material dimensions of being, so as to interface with all the other partners sharing in the process.

The earthly cosmos uses the language of the cosmograms to manage and lead the countless life processes of earth. The cosmograms make it possible for the elemental beings to 'understand' their tasks for the care and maintenance of planetary life and, in attunement with earth's wholeness, stimulate their activity. The 'crop circles' which have emerged world-wide in the last decades are examples of such cosmogramic writing. They display an astoundingly high degree of geometric precision. The crop circles come about through a lightning-fast interior process which bends the grain stalks so completely — using a biological process — that they are laid in regular fashion next to each other on the ground. This process makes a sign which can easily be read from the stalks which remain standing.

If one does not know the universal language of archetypal patterns, one can be readily inclined to regard the crop circles as hoaxes of human origin, or ascribe their appearance to

---

1 Admittedly, after the first crop circles emerged, some people felt called upon to make similar circles in the grain.

Crop circle at Barbury, Wiltshire, England
on April 20, 1997.

certain mysterious intelligences in space-ships[1].
I have myself visited some crop circles in England and tested their authenticity. My opinion is that they come into
being from within the earth, and their purpose is to make
people aware that with Earth we are dealing with a highly
intelligent organism, with whom communication would
present relatively few problems.

One can imagine that people of the ancient cultures,
who were more sensible of the subtle dimensions of Earth,
could perceive the invisible cosmogramic language of the
countryside and landscapes where they lived. They developed their written characters using the images of the cosmic picture language. The original scripts of mankind arose
in this way, and these often display the same symbols which
we know from aerial photographs of the crop circles. The
Aramaic language too, which Jesus spoke, belongs to those
original languages which were based on the archetypal patterns. A language of this sort has many layers. The spoken
words are accompanied by cosmograms in the invisible
realm. These mediate those aspects of the message which
cannot be conveyed by the layer of linear speech. For this
reason I have suspected that one can find the basic archetypal patterns, i.e., the cosmograms, in the gospel texts —
in so far as they are a true and faithful reflection of Jesus'
words. One of Jesus' sayings has even been handed down in
which he indicates the secret of the invisible archetypal pattern to his disciples.

Jesus said, "When you see your likeness, you rejoice. But
when you see your images which came into being before
you, and which neither die nor become manifest, how
much you will have to bear!" (Tm, Log. 84).

By the term 'your likeness' is meant that dimension of
reality which one can see with one's physical eyes. This is
contrasted with the archetypal images which lie beyond linear time: they have arisen before us, they do not pass away
and they belong to the invisible dimension of reality. With

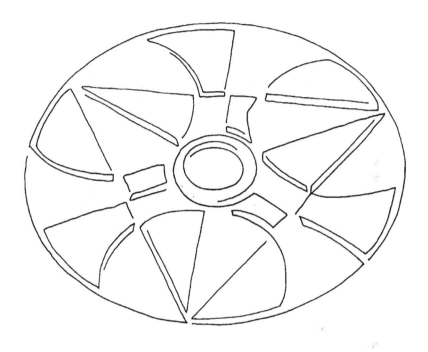

Crop circle at Winterbourne, Wiltshire, England,
on June 1, 1997.

his final statement, Jesus refers to the power of spirit and soul which dwells within these archetypal images.

My first efforts to find the archetypal patterns in the four gospel texts were catastrophic. Everywhere I saw nothing but a gray veil of mist which remained completely opaque. Then, on November 14 1996, a dream came to my aid: I was en route to the mountains to climb with a friend. We hurried to catch a bus. When we arrived at the top, I saw a wine press there. Positioned in the middle of the press machinery were two finely ground, circular stones. At first glance they seem to fit perfectly together. However, as I walked around the press, I noticed a place where they gaped apart so that a crack showed.

I made myself very small and crept through this crack. And so I came into an inner room which resembled a museum. Preserved in it were the most beautiful artworks from different periods of human history. I noticed that only works with a religious content were kept there. I well remember one group of beautiful statues of the Buddha fashioned from white porcelain.

When I came back later to admire the art again, the museum was completely empty. I realized that in the meantime robbers had broken in and carried everything away. I was much distressed. Then I became aware of a voice which advised me to see the vanished artworks in the mirror of my memory. The dream ended with my passing once more through the empty rooms of the museum and bringing back to my memory every absent work of art. At the very moment that its form arose within me, it was back again in its original place and visible to the external eye. The rooms of the museum were filling up again and I rejoiced exceedingly.

When I awoke, it was immediately clear to me that the dream had to do with my difficulties in reading the archetypal pattern in the four gospel texts. The first part indicated how I might find a place in the text which gave access to

*Crop circle at Alton Priors, Wiltshire, England,
on July 11, 1997.*

the plane of its archetypal images. I should make myself aware of scarcely noticeable, illogical connections within the texts. In those places there would be a sort of gate to open the hidden archetypal patterns.

The purpose of the second part of the dream, dealing with the art treasures, was to confirm that the cosmogramic patterns did exist within the gospel texts. The third part showed why they were not perceptible today. Where I would have expected them, my inner sight could perceive nothing but the gray mist.

The image of the robbers breaking in and stealing the art treasures is a reference to people's frequent misuse of the four Gospels over the past 2,000 years, citing them as a pretext to attack peoples of other beliefs and make them suffer. While the texts were being used for the construction of ecclesiastical and worldly power, their inner power was drained away and their archetypal patterns became largely confused.

The last part of the dream showed me a possible way to reconstruct the lost archetypal images. I should view them in their original condition within the mirror of my memory. What was meant here by art treasures was the condition of the gospel texts on their archetypal plane before they fell victim to misuse.

Through deep meditation, sinking into the very being of the dream, I had been able to clarify its message. But I had as yet no inkling how I might carry out the proposed investigation. I tried this method and that, without achieving any real success.

A whole month went by and then I found the book, *The Jesus Papyrus*[2], in a Cologne bookshop. It is about three small fragments, each only a few centimeters square, which

2 Carsten Peter Thiede and Matthew d'Ancona: *The Jesus Papyrus*, Weidenfeld and Nicholson, London 1996; also published as *Eyewitness to Jesus*, Doubleday, New York 1996; and in German as *Der Jesus-Papyrus*, Luchterhand Verlag, Munich, Germany 1996.

have been preserved in the library at Oxford University in England. On them are parts of the Gospel according to Matthew in Greek. What is exciting is that, according to investigations by the authors, the fragments were written between 50 and 70 AD, that is during the time when eye-witnesses of the events still lived in Palestine. The three fragments must therefore reflect the original condition of the gospel message before it was corrupted by misuse.

Fortunately, the three fragments are copied in facsimile on the inside of the book cover. Thus my inner sight could view their etheric layers and I could confirm for myself that they were really uncontaminated and in order. There were gospel texts whose archetypal pattern I particularly wanted to investigate. I took photocopied sheets of these texts and laid them on the papyrus fragments, so that I could examine them in the 'mirror' of the pure power structure of the fragments. The attempt succeeded! The cloud lit up, and I could see the cosmograms which the dream had confirmed.

As an example of the work which followed, I would first like to tell of my investigation of a chapter in Mark's gospel which to the outer eye displays certain illogical, even confusing elements. The relevant section of the chapter carries the title, "The Yeast of the Pharisees and of Herod" (Mark 8:14). It tells how Jesus was going in a boat to the farther shore of a lake with his disciples. Then the disciples realized that they had forgotten to buy bread before their departure and became very concerned. Instead of calming them, Jesus spoke to them in words which had no apparent connection with their concerns. He said, "Keep your eyes open; look out for the yeast of the Pharisees and the yeast of Herod." The disciples went back to worrying about the lack of bread. Then the Master became angry and launched into a vehement speech which still had nothing to do with the disciples' cares about their daily bread. He cried out to them, "Do you still not understand, still not realize? Are

your minds closed? Have ye your heart yet hardened?" The
sentence which tells of the disciples' worries about the lack
of bread is underlaid with the image of a muddy whirlpool
of water leading down into the depths. This image is
accompanied by a feeling of fear and insecurity. With his
warning about the leaven of the Pharisees and Herod, Jesus
has obviously reacted to this invisible whirlpool and not to
the outer cause of the disciples' worry. His warning words
are underlain with the image of a closed bronze ring. The
ring is richly ornamented and covered with a thick green
patina.

Taken in conjunction with Jesus' words about the leav-
en of the Pharisees and Herod, the ring symbolizes the
covenant which the Jews made with God at the foundation
of their religion. Jesus points to this covenant, warning that
it has been twisted by a religious (Pharisaical) and worldly
(Herod) power elite. Instead of linking believers to the
divine power, they have been drawn into a magic ring and
subliminally misused for the purposes of the two elites.
This is the deeper cause of the worry which Jesus had
sensed among his disciples. They were simple Jews of the
people and unconsciously concerned about the spiritual
fate of their countrymen. Without realizing it, they were
reacting to the trap into which their religion had fallen.

Jesus offers the solution to their concern and suggests
how the decadent spiritual situation can be corrected. He
continues: "Have you eyes and do not see, ears and do not
hear? Or do you not remember? When I broke the five
loaves for the five thousand, how many baskets full of
scraps did you collect?' They answered, 'Twelve.' And when
I broke the seven loaves for the four thousand, how many
baskets full of scraps did you collect?' And they answered,
'Seven.' Then he said to them, 'Do you still not realize?'" It
appears the question remained unanswered.

When I stand before this section of text and contemplate the plane of its archetypal image, I get the exalted feel-

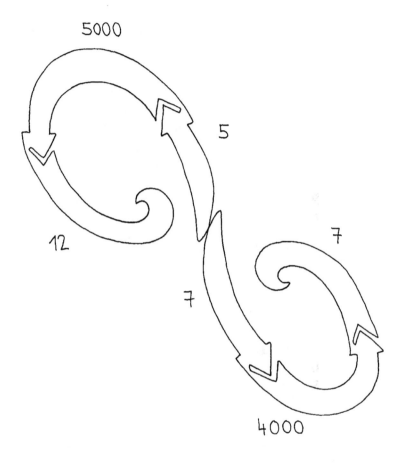

5000

5

12

7

7

4000

The archetypal image of the new covenant
which lies hidden behind Jesus' words
about the feeding of the four and five thousand.

ing that I am standing before the dedication of a new covenant between Humanity and God. At the place where Jesus speaks of the feeding of the five thousand, a leftward-bending spiral begins to manifest which leads in a broad bow upward from its starting point. At the place where he mentions the feeding of the four thousand, a second bow forms. This proceeds outward from the same point and also runs in a bow, but leads in the opposite direction downwards. And so before my inner eye there arises an open lemniscate which unfolds in the rhythm of the numbers named by Jesus.

This cosmogram which arises before our inner eye contains the reason for Jesus' works at the beginning of our era. Jesus has offered humanity a key, and with its help we can reunite ourselves both with the macrocosmic dimension of the divine and with the microcosmic dimension of our earthly world. Humanity stands at the departure gate of both lemniscate bows which run off symmetrically 'upwards' and 'downwards'. They represent the character of the new covenant which is well-balanced within the Universal Whole. It is one where the earthly and spiritual aspects of the human being shall have an equally valued part. Of special note is that, in contrast to the closed ring of the old covenant, the dynamic of the new ring remains open. Humanity is a being whose will is free and we cannot be robbed of this divine gift.

There is another example. It relates to the question posed by 'the rich young man'. The story is recounted in Luke (18:18), Mark (10:17) and in Matthew too (19:16). This man asked Jesus what he must do in order to gain eternal life. The Master replied that he should follow the commandments, such as, 'you shall not commit adultery; you shall not kill; you shall not steal;' and so on. The man replied that he had followed all these commandments from his youth up and wanted to know what he still lacked. Hearing this, Jesus advised him to sell all that he had and

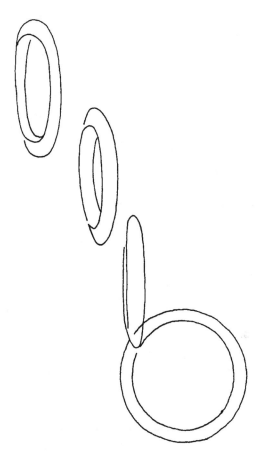

The archetypal image which is hidden
behind the story of the rich young man.

give the money to the poor. "But when he heard this he was overcome with sadness, for he was very rich. Jesus looked at him and said, 'How hard it is for those who have riches to make their way into the kingdom of God! Yes, it is easier for a camel to pass through the eye of a needle than for someone rich to enter the kingdom of God.'"

I have for long been suspicious of the statement contained in the last line. How can Jesus on the one hand affirm that everyone, including the blind and the lame, can share in the kingdom of heaven and yet exclude those who are rich? Inclusion in the kingdom is surely a question of a person achieving a spiritual quality which is independent of material circumstance. However, my investigation into the four etheric layers confirmed that this saying of Jesus is authentic. This fact is cause enough to conclude that the words hide a message which diverges from the logic of what was outwardly spoken. It follows that we have here one of those above-mentioned 'cracks' through which one can 'slip' into the text's archetypal plane.

Following the indications contained in my dream of November 14 1996, I reached behind the sentence about the camel and the eye of the needle and saw a narrow vertical ellipse which really did resemble a needle's eye. At first I was disappointed for I could perceive nothing more than what Jesus' words had already expressed. Then I noticed that the ellipse was turning quite slowly on its axis. The rotation continued until the ellipse had become so slender that I could see only a vertical line stretching upwards and downwards.

The story of the rich young man continues, "Those who were listening said, 'In that case, who can be saved?' He replied, 'Things that are impossible by human resources are possible for God.'" At this point in the text I saw a perfectly rounded circle which was turning clock-wise, and not around its vertical axis.

When the three images of the archetypal pattern are

considered together, they would appear to convey the message that the one-sided character of an exclusively ego-driven development can bring humanity into an extremely dangerous situation. Human beings can gather monstrous power through egocentric development and achieve supremacy over the environment. However, such an ambitious concentration on a one-sided course of development can very quickly turn into its opposite, for its upward path is the same as leads downwards. The accumulated power is obstructed and prevented from flowing in its natural circle, and so ends by working destructively on the originator of the obstruction.

To substitute for the egocentric path, Jesus proposes an economy of forces which is based on the principle of the exchange of flows. When a man brings the dammed-up life forces back into the flow of life — this is the image where the accumulated riches are shared with the poor — he follows a cycle in which he receives everything that he needs and on his part lets the others get what they need from him.

I think that this archetypal pattern indicates that Jesus' last sentence quoted above was not rightly understood and therefore erroneously transcribed. Instead of the sentence, "The things which are impossible with men are possible with God," I suspect that the original statement ran, "The things which are impossible for man *alone* are possible *in common* with God."

Verse 4:14 of John's gospel is of interest for the purposes of our investigation. This passage reports Jesus' conversation with a Samaritan woman at a well. The Master first makes reference to the water of the well, saying, "Whoever drinks this water will be thirsty again." Then he adds, "But no one who drinks the water that I shall give him will ever be thirsty again: the water that I shall give him will become in him a spring of water, welling up for eternal life."

The archetypal pattern underlying this section of text is peculiar. At the point where Jesus transfers his attention from the water of the well to the water of spirit, a power emanates from the text and comes towards me. It takes my attention away from my reading of the text, and instead leads within in the direction of my own heart center. In my midst I see a lake of light from which streams a powerful feeling of beauty and joy. When I look around me from this center point, I see that the world all around is suffused by this same quality of light. It is obvious that there is perfect agreement between the cosmogramic pattern and the words pertaining to it. Even more clearly than Jesus' words, the underlying images express his intention to guide the attention of each single person towards their own individual source. The words themselves can leave the reader in some doubt whether they do not present a demand to believe in Jesus as the only source of 'living water'. The images dispel every doubt in this regard. People are rather challenged to believe in the divine identity of their own core being. Jesus describes himself as that being who leads us to the source which wells up in the heart of every single person.

Chapter 4

The Realization
of the Kingdom of Heaven on Earth

My ability to touch into the etheric layers of the gospel texts and view their basic cosmogramic patterns were not the only instruments I had put to use in August 1996 when I was searching for the 'Fifth Gospel'. I had also made use of the opportunity offered me by the angel named Michael. I examined some of Jesus' words in the mirror of the messagesvon the theme of the 'Fifth Gospel' which Ana Pogacnik had received from him.

Messages of this sort are not like simple dictation on the part of the angelic world. Rather, they need the conscious co-operation of the person who accepts the message and brings it into an appropriate logical form. Particularly with Michael, message reception is not a simple matter for Ana. Each inspiration which streams as an impulse from him to her has many dimensions; in other words, it is a statement composed of various aspects. Only a certain aspect of this multi-dimensionality can be taken into consideration in the transposition into linear speech. With each impulse the receiver must decide which of the aspects offered in the message should be picked up in order to retrieve the statements which fit, and then formulate them into a logical sentence.

I have chosen Michael's message of September 29, 1996, as an example of our co-operation with the angelic world in decoding the 'Fifth Gospel' The message runs as follows:

Knowledge and realizations are flowing to you on various planes and in various forms. It is up to your personal decision which of these you accept, which you follow and which you reject, and these decisions are like railroad points on your evolutionary path. You have a multitude of possibilities, but you can choose only one of them and that one will lead you forward. Among the possibilities available are some which suit you exactly; therefore you should choose only from amongst these, and the result of this choice is your life and the path of your evolution.

Life is so fashioned that it is always offering you various possibilities. Each one of these leads to the same goal, but each one by a different path. The decision on which of the possible paths you will travel is up to you.

All the roads you walk along are put together out of 'hard' and 'easy' challenges, tests, obstacles... so that you may achieve new realizations for your self-development and come by messages and information which bring you up to the next step. Life can be compared to climbing a staircase. Some climb faster, others more slowly; however that also depends on the sort of road you are traveling on. It may be that you have decided on a more difficult way, because you know inside yourself that you must go through a particular experience to make the road smoother further on.

Be assured, there is no wrong road. The only distinction lies in the degree of challenge. The only right road is the road you are on at the moment. However, this does not mean that you have no responsibility for the choices you make for your evolution and, in the last analysis, for your own life. If that were not the case, you humans would be no more than feeble shad-

ow figures, without wills of your own, playthings of an overwhelming fate. However, that is not the evolution in which you are collaborators, and which your decisions can affect. You are the ones who lead, you are the ones who decide and guide.

The idea of an absolutely pre-destined fate, meaning that a person can have no influence on the course of his or her own life, is merely an attempt to flee from personal responsibility and from reality. You are caught up in self-pity and make yourselves into creatures who constantly complain about your lives. You not only pity yourselves, you expect pity from others too. You believe that you are being punished by life and have no chance to alter anything that happens. You believe that life has no consideration for you, and you make it out to be responsible for your fate. Life is not horrible; it is you who have no consideration for each other, because you look on life in such a way as to evoke your self-pity. Such a hostile attitude leads you along a path towards precisely these sorts of experiences.

Nonetheless, you hold onto the idea that you are the absolute masters of your fate. There can be no truth in this, for you know neither your objectives nor your common direction. It is your own soul which guides you, because in the past it has gathered and stored experiences, and it knows the objective towards which you should be going.

There is a middle version which is the right one. You give yourself to life on a road which represents the common direction. You come with a task and an objective which you wish to realize. However, there are different possible ways to reach it. Often you find yourself at a place where the ways part, and there you are required to commit yourself where and when to go onward. And on this decision depends the whole course of further evolution.

Of course, it is true that part of the 'plan' is already laid down at the moment of birth, and there is no possibility of avoiding this fact. That is a person's 'fate', a life-long pattern which you must follow, quite independent of whether you are in a situation where you can follow your path and develop yourselves further, or are caught in a vicious circle and unable to find a way out to lead you forward.

If it were true that fate decided everything, then you'd each find yourselves today at the same stage of development, all mankind would be 'equal'. It is just as incorrect to say that life is good to some and not to others, or that the higher powers love some and not others. You are all beloved, you all have the same value, you are all equally important.

This demonstrates the important role which the subjective element plays in evolution. It is the subjective element which decides on the course of a life. It is worth internalizing the fact that your decisions play an important and responsible role in your evolution. It may be a cause of some anxiety that it depends on every person whether they understand how to use the information which comes to them and so take a step further, or whether they keep turning in circles because they are afraid to make changes in their lives and in themselves. On that depends how much you carry over from a life and how much of it you can take with you on your forward path. You yourself can spoil your chance of reaching the next step quickly.

Not to be overlooked, especially in the last paragraph of the message, is the parallel to the 'parable of the talents', of which Matthew writes in the 25th chapter of his gospel.

This belongs to a group of parables in which Jesus tries to illustrate the concept of the kingdom of heaven. He says that the kingdom of heaven is like a man who is going on a journey and calls his servants together to entrust them with his possessions. "To one he gave five talents, to another two, to a third one; each in proportion to his ability[1]." And then he left the country.

The first section of the parable concerns the different preconditions which individuals bring with them at their birth for purposes of their life's path. These preconditions are given us like 'silver money', so that with the help of this inheritance we can devote ourselves to the task which confronts us. Because we stand upon different steps of our personal development, we receive differing amounts of talents for our journey. One servant receives five, another two, and the third only one talent of silver money for the road.

Referring back to the above quoted message from Michael, the parable discusses that aspect of human life which can be compared to a previously laid down general plan. It represents one's so-called 'fate', a pattern which a person unconsciously follows from day-to-day. Referring to the corresponding part of the message, it is "a pattern which must be followed life long, quite independent of whether a person is in a situation where they can follow their path and develop themselves further, or are caught in a vicious circle and unable to find a way out to lead them forward.

In harmony with this statement as to one's 'fate', the parable of the talents carries on to report how the individual servants dealt with the talents entrusted to them. The one who received the five talents immediately began to trade with them and so gained a further five; the one who had received two added another two. "But the man that had received one went off and dug a hole in the ground and hid his master's money." When the lord returned many

---

1 A talent is an old measure for a precious metal such as gold or silver.

years later, he praised and richly rewarded the two competent servants, but reprimanded the third. Even the one silver talent which this one had kept untouched was taken
away from him and given to the one who had already been
so richly recompensed.

The servant who was reprimanded himself suggests how
to understand the lord's attitude to him: "'Sir,' said he, 'I
had heard that you were ... reaping where you had not
sown, and gathering where you had not scattered.'" This
statement is to be understood as meaning that a person's
subjective contribution corresponds to what is harvested
without having been sown, or gathered without being scattered. Through the creative use of the possibilities offered
by the pattern of our fate, we produce a multiplier which
was not defined in our life's original pattern. Amazingly, we
find a harvest in a place where we have sown no seed. We
are free to deal so imaginatively with our life's affairs that a
new creation arises which is our individual contribution to
the riches of the universe.

Michael's words convey that our "decisions represent a
very important and responsible element of evolution. This
may sound alarming, but it is not meant to be; it is up to
every single person whether they understand how to use the
experiences, information and so on which are offered them
so as to take a further step in their evolution, or whether
they keep revolving on one and the same point because
they are afraid of changes in their own lives and in themselves."

Unfortunately, people have understood the parable of
the talents, as recorded by the writer of Matthew's gospel,
in precisely the sense against which Michael's message
warned; namely, that of inspiring fear. The parable ends
with that repetitive pattern, already so often mentioned,
whose etheric layers do not support as being Jesus' words:
"As for this good-for-nothing servant, throw him into the
darkness outside, where there will be weeping and grinding

of teeth." So the text ends with a curse on those people who are not capable of perceiving the opportunities which life offers them.

Instead of allowing the man the freedom to decide for or against life's offerings, and therefore make mistakes, he is handled here as one might deal with a minor child who is judged guilty if he does not increase his lord's goods. The parable's true conclusion takes place a verse earlier. There the emphasis is placed on the meaning of dealing creatively with one's talents: "For to everyone that has will be given more, and he will have more than enough; but anyone who has not, will be deprived even of what he has." The theme of dealing creatively with what life offers you is carried further in three other parables about the kingdom of heaven, all three of which — one following the other — exhibit a nearly identical structure. (Mat 13:44-50).

In the first, the kingdom of heaven is compared to a treasure buried in a field, "which someone has found; he hides it again, goes off in his joy, sells everything he owns and buys the field." In the second, the kingdom of heaven is "like a merchant looking for fine pearls; when he finds one of great value he goes and sells everything he owns and buys it." In the third, the kingdom of heaven is "like a drag-net that is cast in the sea and brings in a haul of all kinds of fish. When it is full, the fishermen haul it ashore." They find many small fish in the net and among them there is one good, large fish. All the small fish are thrown back into the sea and without further thought they choose the large fish[2].

On October 6, 1996, Ana received a related message from Michael, the first part of which states as follows:

> *Your life has more meaning than merely to satisfy the needs of your body, soul and spirit. Life is a schooling, and at the same time it is the best teacher, leading you through different situations and tests so that you can gather the information and experiences*

*which you need for your personal growth.
Consequently, the meaning of life consists in the constant learning and acceptance of information, so that
you can grow and unfold yourself. Life is to be looked
on as a gift which is given you so that you can learn
something on your earthly path, and not as a vale of
tears which must be suffered through. Your attitude to
life is of the utmost importance, because through it
you are either called on to grow, or there is a brake
put on it. As I have already told you, the path which
your life takes is dependent on your own decision and
choice; because this is so, the sort of relationship you
have with life and how you regard your life is
absolutely decisive.*

*Each one of your lives leaves behind it a general
message on which you have been working throughout.
To be more precise, you are busy with it during your
whole life, with the help of different experiences and
realizations ... forming this message. You imbibe the
information helpful to your development through a
whole lifetime, both in the personal and in the super-
personal realms involving the evolution of humanity
and civilization respectively. The reason that every
life is so valuable and inestimable is because you have
the chance to learn and grow through it.*

*Learn to contemplate life in its many layers and
also as a whole. That helps you to recognize the crimson thread which runs through it. This crimson
thread also helps you to gain a better overview of the
events which come to pass. Above all, it will help you
to avoid involving yourself in trivia. It too often happens that you get involved in or become concentrated*

---

2 (Translator's note). The concluding two sentences of this paragraph are taken
from a parallel version of the parable which is found in the Gospel of Thomas
(Tm, Log. 8).

on events which, from the perspective of wholeness, have only fringe importance. In this way your strength is unnecessarily dissipated, and too often your zest for life as well. It is certainly true that every event in which you involve yourself is important and does hide some information within it, but you should learn to contemplate life as a wholeness and always follow its crimson thread. Otherwise you are just a lost being who wanders to and fro, headless, on the chess board of earth.

The treasure which is buried in the field of daily life stands for the realizations and pieces of information which are hidden in our life's web. One should continuously be on the lookout, searching for the area of the life situations streaming towards us where 'the pearl of great value' may appear. A person shows good sense when they decide to act only on the opportunity which leads their life's crimson thread forward, leaving to one side all the other possibilities offered them. In this way a person resembles the wise fisherman who threw the little fish back in the water and, without further thought, chose the big one. He knew that one fulfills one's task when one always decides to take the step which takes one further forward without any detours, instead of losing oneself in the countless possibilities which life offers.

Unfortunately the writer of Matthew's gospel has once again concluded the third parable of the kingdom of heaven with a damning judgment. First of all, he has divided the fish which were caught into good and bad. Then comes the statement which we have seen so often and which, judged by its etheric layers, is a foreign body within the organism of the gospel: "This is how it will be at the end of time: the angels will appear and separate the wicked from the upright, to throw them into the blazing furnace, where there will be weeping and grinding of teeth."

Fortunately, the manuscript of the Gospel of Thomas, which has already been mentioned as discovered in the desert of Nag Hammadi, has preserved the original version of the parable about the wise fisherman. It reads: "The man is like a wise fisherman who cast his net into the sea and drew it up from the sea full of small fish. Among them the wise fisherman found a fine large fish. He threw all the small fish back into the sea and chose the large fish without difficulty. Whoever has ears to hear, let him hear." (Tm, Log. 8).

The concept of the dualism of good and bad, evoked by the string of parables about the kingdom of heaven in the gospel according to Matthew, has misleading effects. It creates the impression that participation in the kingdom of heaven depends on a person's obedience to the rules which Jesus' teaching may have established. One gets impression that the kingdom of heaven is a far away kingdom that is reserved for the 'good' and is closed to the 'bad'. The kingdom of heaven — also translated in many places as the kingdom of God — is thereby elevated far from Earth and from our daily life.

This impression is contradicted by Michael's message, which in marked fashion concentrates precisely on the web of daily life. Message after message which Ana has received from him refers to the fact that the earthly life of incarnated man, when rightly understood and perceived in all its ramifications, contains the quality of the kingdom of heaven. Those of Jesus' sayings about the kingdom of God which are not veiled in the form of a parable also confirm this same outlook on earthly life.

Two of these are of special interest. Chapter 17 of Luke's gospel includes a saying which is also confirmed by the discovery at Nag Hammadi (Tm, Log. 113). Luke's gospel reads, "The coming of the kingdom of God does not admit of observation and there will be no one to say, 'Look it is here! Look it is there!' For look, the kingdom of God is among you." (Luke 17:20).

The message is even more precise in Jesus' words handed down in Logion 3 of the Gospel of Thomas: "If those who lead you say to you, 'See, the Kingdom is in the sky,' then the birds of the sky will precede you. If they say to you, 'It is in the sea,' then the fish will precede you. Rather, the Kingdom is inside of you, and it is outside of you...."

The first part of the Logion picks up and more precisely defines the words quoted above from Luke's gospel. The 'kingdom of God' is neither to be sought in heaven nor is it to be found in relationship to earthly affairs. Human beings are required to find it in their being and doing, in the here and now. Obviously it is a dimension of daily reality which people usually overlook. In order to define the conditions which determine the presence or absence of the qualities of daily life described as 'heavenly', the passage continues further, "... when you come to know yourselves, then you will become known and you will realize that it is you who are the sons of the living Father. But if you will not know yourselves, you dwell in poverty and it is you who are that poverty."

For us to perceive the life within us and around us as banal, superficial and one-dimensional reflects on our personal attunement. If we do not strive for an exchange with the divine core of our being, if we do not commit ourselves to the search for the deeper meaning of our lives, if we are not ready to develop a sensitivity which corresponds to the subtle components and ramifications of life's web, then the quality of our daily life is indeed poor, and we imagine ourselves to be in the middle of an impoverished — that is to say an alienated — world. And *vice-versa*, daily life can be a way of initiation into the secrets of Being if we make ourselves consciously aware of the signs contained in all of life's occurrences and deal creatively with them.

This does not just concern the far-reaching enrichment or impoverishment of the personal life. Since we human beings are part of the communal organism of humanity, the consequences of our individual attitudes to life impress themselves on the state of humanity's communal quality of life. At the present time, this is characterized by poverty and waste, warfare and planetary pollution. And vice-versa, the more men turn to the path of personal change, making themselves sensitive to the earth and trying to manifest their newly won capacities and realizations in daily life, the more the earth will become the kingdom of heaven. To state this concretely, it would mean that we could live in a world that made possible the general development and perfecting of all the parts composing its Wholeness, without the development of individual persons or presences, realms of being or dimensions of space being limited, obstructed or simply excluded.

Another more detailed insight into the interconnections between the individual and the communal is given in the first transmission which Ana received from Michael on September 15, 1996. This vividly portrays the key role of self-recognition, which Jesus emphasized in Logion 3:

> *Each person's life is like a little piece in the mosaic of the whole of evolution, of the whole of humanity; and not only of humanity but of creation too. For this reason, everyone is important, as is every personal path and the development of each individual person, because the whole evolution (of humanity and of the universe) depends on everyone. Every person represents a part of the total evolution — not just a passive but an active part. Every individual contributes, through their life, their deeds, their steps, their whole development... a part of the total evolution. This is a message of great significance, or to put it another way, it is important for all of you to make yourselves conscious of it, so that you have a more responsible awareness of your life and your personal unfolding. There are many layers in this and those who hinder*

their own development and deny themselves permission to grow, hinder not only themselves but also put the brakes on progress in general.

This is not about threats. That is certainly not my intention because I know that threats do not offer an appropriate path to success. I would only like to say that there are people who are too little conscious of the importance and value of every single person, of what wealth you carry within you and how necessary you are. At the same time, you should make yourselves aware what portentous influence you can have (on evolution) and how far-reaching is your influence on the Wholeness. What strength you carry unconsciously within you!

It is most important for you to know that in the first place you work totally as individuals, and only in the second place as individuals who are joined together in a wholeness. Too often you forget to be aware of yourselves as individuals and instead seek to blend into the crowd. In this way you avoid and flee from your responsibilities. In doing so, you lose yourself, your strength and your identity.

The first absolute necessity is for you to make a tightly locked unity of yourselves, in order to integrate into a greater Wholeness. As a unity, this again can be part of a still greater Wholeness. If just one little part of these interconnecting unities is weak and becomes unfastened, if it does not stay within its own stream and on its own path, the Wholeness can break apart.

In short, every person must first take care for themselves and for their own development; as long as you are not capable of doing that, you can go no further. Nobody expects you all to work in the same way. You humans stand on different evolutionary steps, on

different planes, and everyone must follow this evolu-
tionary law. For this reason, everyone has a task
which corresponds to their stage of development.
Nobody expects all of you to reach the same stage of
development. It is the magic of Wholeness that there
are unlike parts which make connections with each
other for their mutual help and enrichment.

The meaning of the whole of evolution is con-
tained in your joining with each other and exchang-
ing the gifts which you mutually need. Life is perfect,
just as the cosmos of which you are part is perfect. In
the same way you yourselves are perfect, with this dif-
ference only, that you are not conscious of it, or do not
want to admit it.

Chapter 5

Traces of the Feminine and the Voice of Nature in the Gospels

If it is true, as suggested in the last chapter, that Christ's message is closely connected to the lives of people in their earthly incarnations, how can we reconcile the gospels' paucity of information about the Feminine, Earth and Nature? We are standing on the threshold of a 21st century which insists on the social equality of woman — as measured by the man's role — and it is not easy for us to accept the patriarchal orientation of the gospel texts and their defective environmental consciousness. These deficiencies challenge the universal significance of Christ's message.

Jewry in the time of Jesus was such a patriarchal society that life there must have placed severe limitations on his attempt to reach out to humankind. Even if he had wanted, he could not have directly addressed the feminine side of Humankind and of the Divine because the necessary level of understanding was lacking. On the other hand, we must ask whether some of Jesus' sayings may not be related to feminine concerns and have come down to us in the form of parables, intended to reach women by way of their feelings. Daily life was also regarded as worthless in the culture of his people, and yet our investigations show that Jesus succeeded in communicating about it, although in coded form.

In the first chapter I made mention of my capacity to

perceive the elemental world and converse with the consciousness of Earth and Nature. I made use of this potential to trace the feminine aspects of Christ's message and get a feeling for the role which Earth and Nature play there. However, throughout the whole spring and summer of 1997 there was no time to give to the matter. My days were packed full of journeys, seminars, lectures and earth-acupuncture business. It was not until one full year after the original inspiration to commit myself to the search for a Fifth Gospel that I had my first opportunity. Once again I was on the small rocky island in the Adriatic where I regularly retire each year to review my personal development and prepare for future tasks. For some years I had conducted 'conversations' there with two highly developed elemental beings who have access to the wisdom of earth's systems. One is a being of the air element, a fairy who ensouls a tiny olive grove in which I work by day. The grove consists only of three olive trees, which however cast a sufficient shade for me to be able to meditate and write.

The other being I call the 'Old Wise One'. His focal point is at the edge of a stony hollow on the peak of the island's central hill. In my experience such a being has a special role within the common consciousness of Earth. This is to preserve the memories and wisdom which the earth systems have acquired through eons of evolution and make them available as needed to other beings in the area for which he is 'responsible'. His role had made his help exceptionally important to my efforts to bring home the world of elemental beings to the consciousness of present-day people. In past summers I had often communicated with him in this context and, quite exceptionally, I even know his name; he is called Julius, the Old Wise One.

The communication which runs to and fro between us cannot be described as conversation in the usual sense. Rather it is an exchange of feelings which flow between us in deep silence. The consciousness of nature knows no log-

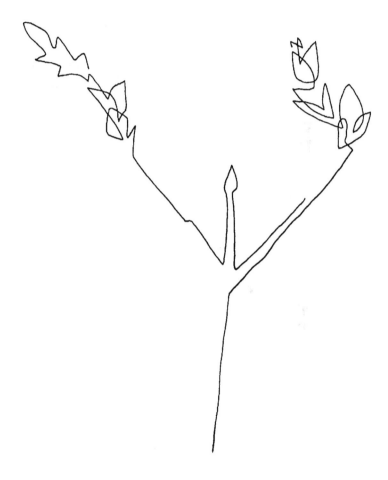

ical thinking based on the linear formulation of words, but exists instead in the form of a rounded wholeness which can best be compared to the way in which we humans exchange our feelings. Consequently the process which transfers thoughts into the vibrations of feeling is decisive for mutual understanding.

To begin the dialogue I sink down into my place of inner repose and concentrate on the core of my being. From that place, I open myself to my partner and ask whether he is ready for the exchange. His readiness is usually conveyed to me by a sense that the 'feeling atmosphere' of the ambiance around me is becoming much denser and more concentrated. When I sense that permission is given, I formulate my question in the form of feelings and imaginations and let them stream out into space. This cannot happen by force of will, but is easily accomplished by the warmth and directness coming from the strength of one's heart. Then begins a process where I transfer the answer, which streams towards me in the form of pictures and feelings, into a logical form. I quickly write this down in a notebook which I always carry with me.

Elemental beings have a wealth of knowledge accumulated from the whole of earth evolution. But when we converse with them about gospel texts, we must ask, do they also have insights into the secrets of human cultural creativity? The answer can only be an emphatic 'yes'. It is an illusion to believe that our thoughts and consequently our feelings occur as if in empty space. This simply cannot be, because to complete our thought processes we must use the earth-bound systems which interconnect our brain and nerves. So all that has happened on earth up till now is kept in the memory of the common consciousness of Earth. Naturally, these include the events which happened in Palestine on the threshold of our era, together with the mistakes which accompanied their transcription into the gospel texts.

The conversation with the fairy of the olive grove took place around four o'clock in the morning on September 22, 1997. I had already lain awake for a long time, feeling that an experience was coming to me but having no idea how to approach it. I decided to grope my way through the darkness to the olive grove and there listen in the silence. This proved to be the right thing to do. The atmosphere was compressed by the presence of a sweetly radiant being. The characteristic vibrational pattern of the fairy mistress of the olive grove was unmistakable.

Seizing the opportunity offered me by her invitation, I put the question which most troubled me out into the space around me. "Can one find traces in the gospels of the Earth Mother, that is, of a feminine component?" The answer came to me in the next moment and left no doubt that it was positive. First, my attention was guided to the well-known parable of the lilies of the field, where Jesus says: "Think how the flowers grow; they never have to spin or weave; yet I assure you, not even Solomon in all his royal robes was clothed like one of them." (Luke 12:27). As this story arose in my memory, I saw in it a song of praise in honor of the Earth Mother, who makes so abundantly available what all creatures need for life.

To my regret, I also perceived a dark shadow around the joyful hymn. I asked, "Where is the problem?" In reply, my attention was guided to the verses in which the parable is embedded. At the beginning it says: "...(do not) worry about your life and what you are to eat, nor about your body and how you are to clothe it," (Luke 12:22) and again in conclusion: "But you must not set your hearts on things to eat and things to drink; nor must you worry." (Luke 12:29). The words, "you must not set your hearts on things" and "do not worry" arose in my mind as especially meaningful.

My interest was awakened and I asked for more clarification. In reply came a whole treatise on humanity's relationship to the systems of earth, about which Jesus had taught in his time. Only a few fragments of this teaching have been preserved, unnoticed, in the gospel texts, perhaps because the earthly aspects of life were suspect in the minds of Jesus' contemporaries and the generations which followed. The fairy gave me to understand that there are two basic aspects in the relationship between people and the life systems of earth. These aspects run parallel to each other and yet are interwoven. On the one hand, the earth systems deal with humanity as with all other beings, making available what we need for life. We are cared for no less than is a stalk of grass, a beetle or a flower. We are gifted with a fantastically perfect body, and with the food, water, air and strength to care for it. This sort of relationship represents the Earth Mother's gift to humanity. Earth plays the role of the giver, and we humans the role of receiver and user. This corresponds to a mother-child relationship, where we are like infants suckled by the Earth Mother.

As soon as our soul and spiritual development matures, it is time to change this relationship to an interrelationship, one where we too are givers and supply the life systems of earth with something that provides essential enrichment for the whole earth world. In this way a one-sided relationship is turned into a cycle of mutual exchange.

This part of the communication made me realize that our modern ecological consciousness is an expression of this maturation process. We have matured enough to transcend the role of over-fed infant and transform our one-sided and linear relationship with earth's systems into a relationship of exchange. However, our present ideas of environmental protection and preservation of nature do not go far enough. They usually represent no more than a heightened concern for human survival and do not extend to making a creative contribution towards the enrichment of the earth's systems.

In giving this explanation, the fairy had tried to give me

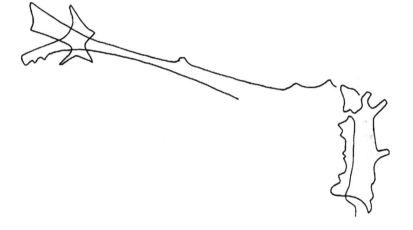

the key to my question about the feminine; also to bring home to me what Jesus had to say about people's relationship with the Earth Mother, using the parable of the lilies in the field. Jesus' command not to trouble ourselves or have any cares came back to me, amplified by verse 25 from the same chapter: "Can any of you, however much you worry, add a single cubit to your span of life?" A related message was pulsating all around me and penetrating my being, but I knew that I still had not understood it. I made a strenuous effort to bring it into some comprehensible pattern.

Way beyond all my efforts, the words were suddenly there. Quickly I wrote them down in my notebook. "Humankind is a source of strength for us Beings of the Earth. When you close yourselves off in cares about your own survival, you dam up the flow of the forces which we need from you to nourish ourselves."

I was moved by this statement, and my mind began to reckon up all the qualities which only we humans possess and which could be invested as capital in the exchange cycle with the earth systems. First there is our capacity to think and decide independently. From this comes the potential to make creations which go beyond the preconceived pattern of what already exists. Yet, for the living beings of earth which participate in the common consciousness of the planet, our capacity to individuate may be still more important. Individual access to the divine core of the universe stands open to us humans, and with it the potential to make our own personal decision to love and serve life.

Jesus' closing words about the lilies conform to this thought. I should like to quote the corresponding verse from the translation by Emil Bock[1], because it better emphasizes the essential part of the statement: "Let your striving be directed to the Kingdom of God, for then everything else will be shared with you." (Luke 12:31). In the

1 The *New Testament*, translated by Emil Bock, Urachhaus, Stuttgart, 1991

last chapter we recognized that the kingdom of God and kingdom of heaven are two names for a way of being on planet earth and do not denote a far-off transcendental kingdom. These findings demonstrate the real meaning of the verse. Jesus is requiring people to express their individual beings within the living processes of earth. In doing so we fulfill what, on their different planes of existence, earth and its living beings need from us. In return we are provided with what we need from earth's systems: we are clothed, kept warm, provided with nourishment, and loved.

We block the ways which give access to the inexhaustible provisions of earth's living forces when we concentrate one-sidedly on questions of survival, or when we fight over resources or from fear of lack pile up giant stores of goods. Then we forget who we are and the meaning of our evolution. And so we pre-program the next step in our self-obstructive course: we feel obliged to use earth violently, to rip what we need from her. This leads to a general impoverishment in the qualities of feeling and to environmental destruction. Our unbelief leads us to think that such circumstances compel us to behave still more heedlessly to satisfy our supposed needs. We grasp at splitting the atom, manipulation of genes, cloning of embryos. We are caught in a vicious circle. In the parable of the lilies of the field, Jesus foresaw man' s future distress and suggested how we might see a holistic relationship with earth's systems.

Next, I asked the fairy of the olive grove about the role of women in the Christian message. In face of the patriarchal norms which doubtless formed the background of Jesus and the evangelists, I asked, could their role at least have been addressed in a general way?

In answer, the story of Jesus' visit to the two women, Martha and Mary (Luke 10:38), arose in my memory. Martha was busy, completely involved in the chores of the household, caring for the physical well-being of Jesus and his many disciples. On the other hand, Mary had seated

herself at Jesus' feet and was listening to him speak. In a
rage Martha complained to Jesus about her sister not helping her with all the work she had to do. Jesus took Mary's
part with the words, "Martha, Martha, you worry and fret
about so many things, and yet few are needed, indeed only
one. It is Mary who has chosen the better part, and it is not
to be taken from her."

I had had little interest in this passage before the
guardian of the olive grove brought it to my notice, always
'skimming over it' without remarking how precisely it
relates to the transformation of women's role in our culture,
a transformation which at that distant time was still dor-
mant.

In the ancient mother-centered societies, the sacred role
of women had comprised the birthing and maintenance of
the life streams of the household. In the following age these
had been relegated to secondary importance. Jesus' meeting
with Martha and Mary expresses the vision for the future
role of women, that of advancing out of the background
role into which the Patriarchate had thrust them, and establishing their sovereign right to occupy themselves in areas
which society had traditionally reserved for men. In this
case it was the area of religion, i.e., the question about the
meaning of Being.

When the fairy noticed that I was somewhat disillu-
sioned by the story of Martha and Mary — because what
then lay in the future had in the meantime been fulfilled —
she recalled another text to my memory. It concerns the
anointing of Jesus by Mary Magdalene, which is reported
by the three evangelists. According to the gospel of Mark,
it happened shortly before Christ's passion. "He was at
Bethany in the house of Simon, a man who had suffered
from a virulent skin-disease; he was at table when a woman
came in with an alabaster jar of very costly ointment, pure
nard. She broke the jar and poured the ointment on his
head. Some who were there said to one another indignant-

ly, 'Why this waste of ointment? Ointment like this could have been sold for over three hundred denarii and the money given to the poor;' and they were angry with her." (Mark 14:3).

Jesus took Mary Magdalene under his protection and justified her action in words which leave no doubt that through his anointing by a woman something of great significance had happened to him: "In truth I tell you, wherever throughout all the world the gospel is proclaimed, what she has done will be told as well, in remembrance of her." (Mark 14:9)

I must add that I do not consider the gospel's explanation of the event to be authentic, even though it is supposed to have been given by Jesus himself. It reads, "She has anointed my body beforehand for its burial." (Mark 14:8). It is certainly true that after the anointing Jesus was betrayed, and soon afterwards seized and crucified. However, the meaning of his passion, suffering and death upon the cross cannot have been comprised in his burial! In his previous predictions of the Passion, it was the *change* which leads from death to resurrection which was emphasized as being the meaning of the whole journey, and not death as such.

However, the fairy of the olive grove invited me to take a yet more differentiated view of the event. The anointing by Mary Magdalene represented the 'incarnation of the feminine principle', necessary before Jesus entered upon his passage through hell. The anointing awakened the feminine or feeling side of his being, so that Jesus could consciously integrate it. Breaking the vessel and pouring the nard over his head symbolized this awakening, because the perfume's sweet smell speaks to the feminine plane of man. The Jews present voiced their fury at the presumed waste of money and squandering of valuable oil, reflecting as in a mirror the taboo touching of the man Jesus by the power of the Feminine.

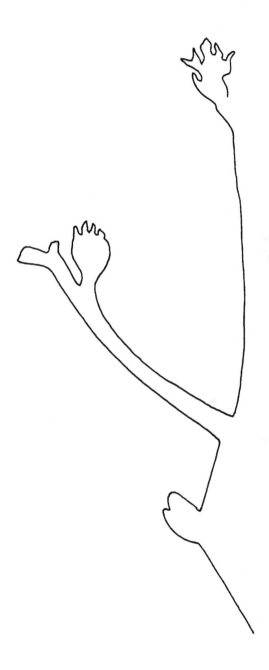

To understand how this event points towards the future, we should know that Jesus sought to lead humanity into their evolutionary future, not only by teaching about it, but by living it, modeling it in advance through his three years of public deeds on earth. Certain key events in his life — and the anointing in Bethany belongs among them — indicate how he traveled ahead of humanity along the path which leads to our future. Behind him he left a track which we can follow today when we search for ways to develop further.

The fairy of the olive grove evoked this wider connection in my consciousness to make me aware of the correspondence between Jesus' anointing in Bethany and his touching into his feminine side. The anointing occurred directly before Jesus had to undergo death upon the cross. When he walked again among his disciples a few days later, after the resurrection, he had a different sort of body. Quite clearly, he had not only gone through death but also through a far-reaching change. His body was 'ethericized', meaning that it certainly showed an earthly quality and therefore was of earth, but it revealed at the same time that it was completely permeated by spirit. The two aspects of the human being which are normally separate — the earthly which is visible externally, and the spiritual which is hidden within — were now united in Jesus, both occupying the same space and the same time. According to the reports in the gospels, he demonstrated the new quality of his presence by entering a room through a closed door to meet with his disciples. Elsewhere they tell us that to prove that he was no spirit, he ate a piece of fish before their eyes.

The fairy told me that in the figure of the resurrected Jesus we see the true likeness of future man, conceived as he will become. We are now going through a process of change. Part of the current phase already lies behind us. It requires a gross materialization of our being and can be compared to the death phase which Jesus underwent . Our

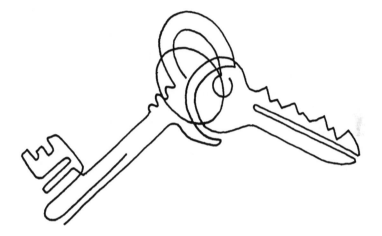

soul and spiritual aspects are repressed into our subconscious and no longer belong to our lives' reality. In the next period of change — and this has proceeded quite far already over the last hundred years — we will learn to make conjoint within ourselves the outer and the inner, the physical and spiritual. Both poles will exist in a balanced wholeness. The result of the change will be recognizable in that our physical aspects will become lighter, i.e., 'ethericized', and on the other hand the soul and spirit aspect will be more deeply joined with earth, meaning that they will be revealed for everyone.

So that humanity can achieve this portentous change, Jesus took over the role of advance man and through his own physical experience preceded us on this three phase path of transformation. He himself was conscious of this task when he declared, in the words of John's gospel: "And when I am lifted up from the earth, I shall draw all people to myself." (John 12:32).

Jesus would not have been able to complete this task — as I understood the fairy — if he had not become conscious beforehand of the extension of his being in the feminine and emotional areas, together with the possibility of integrating them through experience. Such integration requires the incarnation of those forces and qualities which are of absolutely basic significance to the success of the transformation process which we are describing. This is equally true of men and women. Just as the way to self knowledge is open not only to men but also to women — as we saw in the story of Martha and Mary — so the feminine qualities and forces are not reserved for women only. As the anointing by Mary Magdalene teaches, they are equally important for perfecting the masculine side of our being.

I continued my conversation with the fairy of the olive grove in the early hours of the next morning, asking her to show me an example where Jesus places special emphasis on the feminine qualities. In reply, I was led to a powerfully stated passage in Matthew's gospel which speaks about the power of love. It says there, "You have heard how it was said, 'You will love your neighbor, and hate your enemy.' But I say this to you, love your enemies, and pray for those that persecute you; so that you may be children of your Father in heaven, for he causes his sun to rise on the bad as well as the good, and sends down rain to fall on the upright and the wicked alike." (Mat 5:43).

This passage first characterizes the patriarchal understanding of love as resting on the requirement to fulfill society's norms. Such love is understood as a mutual sympathy between the like-minded, and excludes as 'enemies' those whose minds are otherwise. However, Jesus then introduces a new understanding of the concept of love. Love is exalted in its true feminine form; it flows and reconciles, and nobody is excluded from her constant circle.

On November 9, 1997, my colleague Ana received a message from the angel Michael, which has more to say on the matter:

> *Love is really a much wider, more inclusive concept than the wayt you use it. It does not mean only being fond of somebody, or even loving that person, but (it means loving) life itself.*
>
> *Love is a basic component of all that is. It is a sort of atom from which the world that you know is put together. Actually, it is a vibration, and an energy, which possess unbelievable power. Love is the most direct and concentrated power that exists. It is the true life force which shakes one utterly. It moves the heart when someone receives its touch. Love is a light which is capable of embracing you and — however difficult the moment may be — it gives you new strength and new courage. Actually there are no words to describe this beauty, this wonderful world, this gentleness and strength which are all contained in*

love. To put it in few words: Love is Life.

You have no idea how simple and beautiful life can be when you make yourselves able to join in its stream, the stream of life — of love. More than anything else, this requires you to take another view of life and of everything which is bound up with it. New insights and new dimensions of life, closed before, will open themselves up to you. Life really is a play in which you appear in order to learn and gain knowledge, and therefore grow. Then your life will no longer be a tangle of chaotic happenings which you try to guide along specific, pre-conceived routes. The rules by which you live, which you have established over time through tradition, upbringing and civilization, will no longer be so rigid but more relative and less binding.

Chapter 6

Conversations with
the 'Old Wise One'

In the last chapter I introduced Julius as the 'Old Wise One'. My first conversations with him were of a very different character to my conversations with the fairy of the olive grove. I saw in him the opportunity to look at my method of decoding the 'Fifth Gospel' through the mirror of a consciousness which obeyed laws quite other than my own. He belongs to the race of earth elementals, and the highly developed intelligence of 'the Old Wise One' is no less than the expression of the communal consciousness of Earth.

On September 18, shortly before sunrise, I sat beside the stone where Julius focuses his forces and pondered over my work on the gospel texts. In this way I hoped to give him an insight into the structure of my work. After some time I began to sense a returning stream of thought that was building from his side. Immediately I extended all my sensors so as to gain some presentiment of his feelings about my work. After a little while his feelings had so far impressed themselves on my consciousness that I could form them into a complex sentence. He implied, "It is inevitable that people's actions should have a subjective component — and the gospel writings are of course actions — because the independence of every human being is one of the basic laws of your evolution. Because of this, the subjective element is present in all your creative activities. In this sense, the gospels too are not an objective expression of Christ's message, but express the degree to which humans were ready to understand it."

In plain language, this means that the men of the first centuries after Christ chose those aspects which they could best understand out of the many which are contained in the multi-dimensionality of Jesus' works and teaching. These aspects were finally firmly fixed in the four gospels and in Christian evangelism and so handed on to the following generations. One should therefore be aware that the wholeness of Christ's message could not be incorporated, but only those aspects which were best known to the spirit of his epoch and its representatives. This is the subjective element which cannot be avoided. And because it cannot be avoided, no one should be held guilty.

Julius' critical attitude also collided with my own preconceived notion of the 'objective' character of the 'Fifth Gospel'. I had to admit that I had half-consciously cherished the hope that my work on the gospel texts would bring to light the final truth of Christ's message. Contradicting this ideal, Julius advanced the view that I could at most put together a gospel that would restore that part of the message which was optimal for our present time. Even to do that, I must release my half-formed ambitions for the conclusive objectivity of the work. "In your contribution to the understanding of Christ's message, you should not try to veil the subjective component, but quite the reverse, you should present it openly. It would not be wise to deal with this work as your predecessors dealt with it." This was the message he sent me to round off our first conversation.

During the following morning's meditation with Julius, I asked about Christ's relationship to the earth's systems. The first wave of vibrations, bringing me his opinion on the meaning of Christ's power in respect to earth evolution,

showed the very deepest respect. As I understood the Old
Wise One's response, the incarnation of Christ, with all its
various ramifications, is to be seen as the initiation of
humanity onto a new stage of our evolution. A new archetype of the human being was predicated through Jesus. The
new qualities, expressed symbolically in such metaphors as
'immaculate conception', 'without sin', and 'overcoming
death through resurrection', were later conceived as referring exclusively to the life of Jesus; yet, by living these qualities he established an archetype that was suitable for the
life of every individual person who came after him.

Humanity's transition to a new evolutionary stage makes
possible the further evolution of earth's systems because,
since we live on earth, our evolutions are coupled together.
At the old stage of evolution, which for humans is in part
still operative, there was no direct exchange between our
earth-elemental and soul-spiritual aspects. Figuratively
speaking, the old form in which we incarnate on earth has
the appearance of a spiritual figure, which is the soul, riding on a beast. The new stage, initiated by the actions of
Jesus in Palestine, makes possible a more perfect interpenetration of the two poles of our being and so enables an
intensive exchange, in the course of which not only we but
also earth and its living worlds receive essential enrichment.

To be quite honest, I was less interested in Julius' 'theo-
retical treatise' than in 'hearing' some examples from the
gospel texts which would illustrate his views. In reply, he
first referred to the parable of the wicked tenants, which is
reported in three out of the four gospels. The wording in
Luke seems to me to come closest to the original version.
"A man planted a vineyard and leased it to tenants, and
went abroad for a long while. When the right time came,
he sent a servant to the tenants to get his share of the produce of the vineyard. But the tenants thrashed him, and
send him away empty-handed." (Luke 20:9). As I understood Julius' meaning, the beginning part of the parable

presents planet earth as a divine creation, whose holy character humans do not recognize. This is the paradisiacal quality of earth which Jesus described in the concept of the 'kingdom of heaven'. People are closed to this dimension of earth although it represents their true being, and in their narrow mindedness they concentrate on their egotistical needs. Thus we ignore the universal significance of our incarnation on earth.

In consequence many enlightened souls have incarnated in the various cultures of earth to bring home to us the source of our existence here. But, just as the parable tells, we have either silenced these messengers or elevated their sayings to make them the foundation of grandiose religious structures and so alienated them from their true meaning. "But he went on to send a second servant; they thrashed him too and treated him shamefully and send him away empty-handed. Then the owner of the vineyard thought, "What am I to do? I will send them my own beloved son. Perhaps they will respect him."

So happened a unique event in the history of Earth and Humanity. The founding power of the universe — how can one best name it? — the Creator Itself — in the title of this book it is called Christ Power — the Christ Power incarnated on earth among us. For three years he wandered through Palestine, borne in the being and form of Jesus, openly teaching and working, and trying to bring home to men and women the true reasons for their existence on earth.

The parable continues, "But when the tenants saw him they put their heads together saying, 'This is the heir, let us kill him so that the inheritance will be ours.' So they threw him out of the vineyard and killed him. Now what will the owner of the vineyard do to them? He will come to make an end of these tenants and give the vineyard to others."

Julius' commentary on the closing portion of the parable suggested that there was still hope. The repercussions of the crime committed against the son of the vineyard's owner could awaken the lost consciousness of our human wholeness; especially, added Julius, our recollection of the offense over a period of nearly two millennia might accomplish this. The alternative, indicated in the last sentence of the parable, is that the wonderful challenge which over eons has been assigned to Earth and Humankind, will in the future be handed on to another star and another evolution.

Julius chose a second example from the gospels to further illustrate humanity's role within earth's systems. This was the following. "You are salt for the earth. But if salt loses its taste, what can make it salty again? It is good for nothing, and can only be thrown out to be trampled under people's feet." (Mat 5:13).

In these words Jesus has emphasized humanity's significance for the evolution of the *consciousness of Earth*, that is, for the *world of elemental beings*. The human ability to think up unforeseen changes and turn them into decisions is a factor which presents the consciousness of Earth with enormous challenges. By their creative or destructive actions, humans have created unexpected situations in all realms and on all planes of the planet. Willing or unwilling, the intelligence of Earth and Nature must tackle these so that the planet does not lose her balance and plunge into chaos. Challenges of this sort — the destructive parts of which will hopefully be reversed in future — can be unpleasant for the world of elemental beings and the common consciousness of Earth; yet they are welcome because they challenge Earth's intelligence to become more multi-layered and universal.

The saying, "salt for the earth," refers to that human function which imparts an impulse. The alternative saying, "if the salt loses its taste," carries a contrary indication, the danger that the mass of people — then as now — may be prepared to silently give up their inner freedom and spiritual independence and let themselves sink into a lethargic

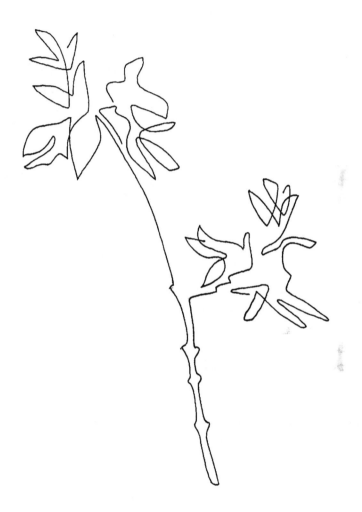

care for daily survival. Then humanity can only wait — here Julius is referring to the last sentence of Jesus' words — until we become a sacrifice to the consequences of our own actions.

On the following morning the Old Wise One directed my attention to the parable of the lost sheep so that I might gain a deeper understanding of the role of the human being. In Luke's gospel this parable follows immediately after the saying about the salt for the earth. Its genuineness is confirmed by the discoveries at Nag Hammadi. According to Matthew's gospel, Jesus told the parable in the following words. "Tell me. Suppose a man has a hundred sheep and one of them strays; will he not leave the ninety-nine on the hillside and go in search of the stray? In truth I tell you, if he finds it, it gives him more joy than do the ninety-nine that did not stray at all." (Mat 18:12).

The nine and ninety sheep which faithfully obey the law of the herd stand for the unawakened persons who are afraid of their own inner potential. They would rather latch onto the mass consciousness and follow established models and stereotypes than be free and responsible for their own decisions. Contrariwise, the one sheep who wanders symbolizes a person's individuation process, and represents a higher stage of our evolution. The road of personal, independent growth cannot be undertaken without the risk that the wayfarer will follow the wrong track, have to tackle unforeseen situations and always be searching.

Julius recommends that the parable should be understood as an emphatic affirmation of the importance of the individuation process of every single person for the further evolution of humanity as a whole; also, how unambiguously the 'Shepherds of Mankind' support one's steps on one's personal spiritual path. This categorical statement was accompanied by an impulse which sought to remind me of the angel Michael's message underlining once again our individual responsibility for our choice of personal path.

According to Julius, we should associate the shepherds who helped the lost sheep with that group of exalted angels who were mentioned in the first chapter as guides and inspirers of humankind's evolution.

Chapter 7

An Essential Step Forward

The most valuable gift which I got from my conversations with Julius, the Old Wise One, were instructions on how to set about reading the inner message in the sayings of Jesus. He suggested that I should take the relevant sayings into my heart and there allow them to dissolve in the power of the heart center, so as to set free the coded elements of the message.

On September 23, 1997, I made my first attempt. Among Jesus' sayings were some whose hidden message had occupied me for a long time. I chose the following, "Can you not buy two sparrows for a penny? And yet not one falls to the ground without your Father knowing. Why, every hair on your head has been counted." (Mat 10:29).

In the first phase I concentrated on my heart center until I could feel the connection with my inner self strongly and clearly. And at that moment it seemed to me that I was looking directly into the eyes of the Christ presence. His presence rose unexpectedly out of my center, identical with my own innermost core of being. I recognized him at once from earlier meetings and could not mistake his unique vibration.

In the second phase I took those words of Jesus I had chosen into my heart center and there allowed their form to dissolve. At the very moment that they disappeared, a return stream began to flow outwards, which my consciousness transferred into words and sentences 'on the way'. I held a writing pad and pencil ready to quickly write down the impressions that were streaming towards me.

When I examined the above-mentioned saying through this translation process, the first sentence which the return stream carried into my consciousness was: "Earthly creation is a wonderful and divine organism." For me at that moment, and for a split second, the world stood still. Fanfares rang out from all four points of the compass, and choirs of joy sounded all around me. It felt as if Earth with all its living riches had waited millennia for a human being to finally speak these words in the name of Christ. The message continued at once, "Within this organism every little piece has its place, its meaning and its role. All pieces of the whole are joined with each other in such a sensitive and universal way that no unforeseen chance can happen. The perfection of the wholeness is so fashioned that its pieces can pick up and embrace each other at any moment. That means that every fear of earth-born humans for their own well-being is superfluous and unfounded. Humanity even has a place of honor among the beings of earth and is the more protected on that account. This is why it is said, "Every hair on your head has been counted."

The whole process — with the message streaming towards me through the inner voice — was a surprise. I felt as if I must be taken by an inner hand and led blindly step by step along a narrow path until the goal was safely reached. There were moments when I expected to topple into the abyss of silence and then in the next instant saw the safety of the onward-leading word.

After this I set myself to translate the sayings of Jesus, one after the other, into a form suitable for the spirit of our age. I have taken most of them from the gospel texts of Matthew, Mark and Luke, after first proving their authenticity — I described my method in the second chapter. Surprisingly, John's gospel yielded little material for the purpose. This is not easy to understand because John's gospel is generally regarded as the one which most directly imparts the traditions left by Christ.

It appears to me that the Gospel according to John was not written based on notes of Jesus' original sayings, taken at the time of his deeds in Palestine, but rather represents the later revelations of Christ. In contrast to the first named gospels, which are called the synoptic gospels and rest on the experiential reports of eyewitnesses, the work of John presents us with messages from Christ. My insight suggests that they were received through direct communication from the presence of Christ after he had passed through death and resurrection. Seen thus, the gospel of John is a backward-looking view of the events in Palestine. Because of the spiritual distance this implies, they hold important insights into the Being of the Christ Power, but in no way need that second distance which I was trying to establish.

In addition to the sayings chosen from the four canonical gospels, I intended to examine all of Jesus' sayings in the Gospel of Thomas, which as already mentioned had been discovered at Nag Hammadi. I could find no reason to doubt their authenticity. However, when I made the connection to the first of these texts and willed to take it up into my heart, a feeling of fear ran through me which clouded all communication. I felt as if waves of violence were overwhelming me, and my whole body trembled. The text dealt with the well-known parable of the leaven which also appears in the canonical gospels. I had thought that the parable's original form would be best preserved in Thomas. There, it runs as follows. "Jesus said, 'The Kingdom of the Father is like a certain woman. She took a little leaven, [concealed] it in some dough, and made it into large loaves. Let him who has ears hear.'" (Tm, Log. 96).

The content of the text could not be the reason for my feelings' strong reaction. I had the same experience when I concentrated on other sayings from Thomas' gospel. What was hiding here?

The Gospel of Thomas is among the writings which were forbidden by the official Church and in the sixth century destroyed down to the last copy. The copy from Nag Hammadi survived the wave of destruction because it was hidden in a huge clay jar away in the desert, together with a number of other Gnostic writings. An Egyptian peasant first discovered the jar by chance in 1945.

The movement which drew its inspiration from the Gospel of Thomas, among other sources, was called Gnosticism. During the first Christian centuries it represented a pole opposite to the official Church. While the official Church organized itself on the model of the power structure of the Roman Empire and finally asserted itself as the Empire's official religion, the interest of the Gnostic movement focused on the path of personal knowledge and valued that. There was rampant and unmistakable tension between the two opposing concepts of Christianity, because the personal path to knowledge which the Gnostics followed needed no confession of faith and no mediating priest. In the end, the conflict with the official Church broke out in violence.

The Gnostic movement's fears of extermination had left behind their traces in the text from Nag Hammadi, and now they confronted me. To overcome this barrier blocking my inner path to the words of Jesus, I made use of my new discovery: I took into my heart the feeling of grief which had overcome me in Thomas' Gospel, and asked my inner self for instructions how to deal with the problem. The answer which I received may be framed in the following words.

In the beginning, Christendom was put together from various streams, each one of which was intended to contribute another aspect to the wholeness of the Christian tradition. The purpose of the tradition is to prepare humanity for the next step of their evolution. Since this step requires diversity, it was not intended that the tradition of

Christ should condense into a unity, but that it should take different forms. As soon as one of these forms or layers is lost, the success of the whole undertaking is brought into question. In corresponding manner, individual, Christ-oriented streams of the early, and in part also of the later, epochs were inspired and set in motion by the Christ Power itself to embody individual aspects of the tradition.

The movement which we describe as Gnostic had the task of cultivating that side of the Christian tradition which emphasizes personal freedom and individual creativity in one's search for the meaning of life. It is an aspect that must be independent of institutional control.

The Gnostics, like other early Christian movements, had their legitimacy, which cannot be denied them. The process which formed the Christian tradition became dangerously unbalanced by the exclusion of the Gnostic schools from the dialogue between the different streams of evolving Christendom, and the movement's final suppression (beginning in the fourth century). In consequence, that aspect of the Christian movement which embodies the striving for community, institutionalization and formal religion became too strong. This had a further consequence from which the Christian tradition still suffers to this day. People who pursue their development through the institutionalized tradition have in the main lost the quality of personal spiritual independence. The unique, subjective relationship to the Godhead is also alien to them. And yet these are qualities which undeniably belong to the Christian tradition.

What can we do now? In the first place, we should forgive both sides in this dispute. The Gnostics were a colorful and complex society, in harmony with the inspiration which they followed. Many of their members did not know the deeper meaning of the movement. Extreme positions were taken and excesses committed which endangered the integrity of the Christian message. And we should forgive the official Church which was not in a position to separate the wheat from the chaff, and in a crude and unchristian way smashed the whole Gnostic movement.

Secondly, we should work to strengthen that side of the Christian tradition which has been drastically weakened by the extinction of the Gnostic stream and of the later movements which tried to play the role of successors. The book before you is in part dedicated to this task, though with no wish to re-awaken the Gnostic tradition. The foremost concern is to make a conscious contribution to restoring the Christian tradition's equilibrium which is out of balance; and at the same time emphasize the components of the individual paths to self-development.

When I had come to understand this point, I lit a candle and spoke my whole-hearted forgiveness to both parties entangled in this unfortunate debate. Afterwards, it proved possible and, for the purpose of forgiveness, desirable, to decipher the sayings from the Gospel of Thomas. Reconciliation between the official Church and the oppressed movements of early and later Christendom is still lagging and to stimulate this, I wish to quote some words from Matthew's gospel. In this passage that very same Peter, the apostle on whom the official Church was founded, comes to Jesus to ask about forgiveness: "…then Peter went up to him and said, 'Lord, how often must I forgive my brother if he wrongs me? As often as seven times?' Jesus answered, 'Not seven, I tell you, but seventy-seven times.'" (Mat 18:21).

After I had overcome the emotional barrier which arose for me personally from the past suppressions of the individual path to knowledge, there soon emerged another hurdle. This became obvious about a week later, after my work had again begun to flow and the inner voice was translating for me easily. The text I was writing down suddenly sounded top-heavy. The influence of intellect, which I had to use for   the   purpose,   had   become   too   strong.

And in consequence the power of the inner voice dried up bit by bit.

So as not to lead myself, and others who trusted in my work, around by the nose, I had set aside three whole months with few interruptions to listen to my inner voice translate Jesus' sayings. At the same time I would devote myself to various phases of my personal change-process. Now I had to free myself from the subliminal rule of my intellectually based thoughts. In my own understanding of life, I had insisted for three decades that the power of the intellect must be balanced by the feeling side, so as to give priority to the voice of the soul and let it be audible through intuition. I well understand how the correct apportionment of these three basic forces is decisive for one's equilibrium, and I try to realize it in my personal life. But every few years it happens afresh that my intellect finds a new and even more refined method to secretly work its way into a dominating role and undermine the balance of the feeling side of my consciousness. It even appears that this is not so much a matter of a personal failing, but rather a pre-eminent task with which people today must incessantly struggle in order that their development may proceed.

Providentially, I had been warned in good time of the danger that my mind would exert a subliminal, lopsided influence on the texts which my intuition was receiving. In the night of September 22-23, the same day that I began translating the sayings of Jesus through my inner voice, I had the following dream: I was inside the vast cupola of a planetarium, busy with building a model of the cosmos. Men were placed at individual focal points of the model, in positions similar to particular stars in the heavens. Their task was to keep their assigned place in the firmament and embody their prescribed roles precisely. I stood on the floor and was in the act of giving final instructions to the men hovering in the heavens above me, so that the model would be perfect.

At this moment one of the participants in the firmament above me went astray. His appearance resembled representations of St. Peter in the art of the Middle Ages. He began to cry out with dreadful shrieks and fly all over the heavens, rocking the established order. My reaction was to become angry. Instead of keeping control of myself and looking around for the cause of the commotion, I began to give orders. In a loud voice, drowning Peter's cries, I commanded him to return to his assigned place.

As long as I remained in dream consciousness, it was easy for me to accept the warning of my soul — my inner self — and see the intellect's subliminal influence in myself, transposed into dream pictures. On the next morning however, as I meditated over the message in the dream, my intellect was awake and did not allow me to understand the warning clearly. I found six different variants to explain the dream message, wrote them carefully down, and tried to act on them immediately. The seventh, the only one not among them, would have proved to be the true one. Unfortunately I only discovered this after a three month long crisis and having gone through all sorts of difficult processes involved in the pursuit of self-knowledge.

It was interesting that it was St. Peter who caused the commotion in the world-model and released my fit of anger: St. Peter, who still usually represents the guarantee of the strength and static order of the official Church. So the message in the dream meant that I had learned to hold the power of my mind fairly well in balance, but that when an extreme situation arises, the mental plane assumes control subliminally. St. Peter's outbreak was an example of such an extreme situation.

In practice, the warning related to certain preconditions which were necessary for me to receive messages through the voice of my heart. In the first place, mind and feeling should be balanced as perfectly as possible; only this would make the voice of intuition audible. In an extreme situation, the unremarked superiority of the mental plane could play a trick on me — as finally happened.

The era in which Jesus lived and worked was the one which laid the foundations for the superiority of intellect today. One can hardly imagine that he would have overlooked the danger to our inner development inherent in such a great disturbance. My insight is that he dealt with this theme in the group of parables in which the figure of the child takes central place. For example, there is the following saying in Matthew: "Unless you change and become like little children you will never enter the Kingdom of Heaven." (Mat 18:3).

The child symbolizes the forces of the immortal soul — which is the evolutionary aspect of man. It is the soul which brings with it through the gate of birth the basic pattern for the development of the individual person in their present life, and seeks to anchor this in their consciousness as they grow. In the process of growing up, there are other aspects of the person's being which step to the forefront. Dominion is claimed by the forces of one's own reason on the one hand and the norms of society on the other, and these work ever more strongly. In contrast, the voice of the soul becomes ever fainter and finally goes under amid the noise of people's daily obligations, thoughts and emotions, taking with it its revelations for life's general plan.

To reflect on the role of the child is the same as reflecting on the original plan written into the memory of one's soul. I have a simple method which I always use to reconnect myself with the soul's original pattern. As soon as I discover that the intellect has again asserted too strong a dominance, I sit down in a quiet place, put all my everyday thoughts and emotions to one side, and give myself over to my heart center. There I remain in the place of rest for quite a long time, without any expectations except to rejoin myself with my own source.

In an especially impressive saying which is related in the

Gospel of Thomas, Jesus describes the way 'back to the child' as the way back to one's own source: "Jesus said, 'The man old in days will not hesitate to ask a small child seven days old about the place of life, and he will live. For many who are first will become last, and they will become one and the same.'" (Tm, Log. 4).

The 'place of life' is equivalent to one's own heart center through which a person can reach the soul as the source of eternal life. The 'many who are first (who) will become last' symbolize the thought patterns which the dominance of intellect in modern man push persistently into the foreground. In the process of rejoining with oneself in the place of rest they will be put in the 'last place'. Then the quiet voice of the 'one and the same', which is the voice of the soul, can be heard and recognized as the original basis of our being.

It would appear that, during the final editing of the gospel texts, those sayings of Jesus which are devoted to overcoming the dominion of the intellect largely fell victims to intellectual manipulation. Rational explanations were added which created the impression that, in his compassion, what Jesus really wanted was a concern for the rights of children. The warning about the dominance of reason was silently ignored.

For example, after he had spoken three sayings one after another on the theme of 'the child', he is supposed to have added, "Anyone who is the downfall of one of these little ones who have faith in me would be better drowned in the depths of the sea with a great millstone round his neck." (Mat 18:6). Apart from the misleading impression which arises from the wording, "who have faith in me," the saying is really an important extension of the message about rejoining with one's own original source. It means that a person who has fallen victim to the misleading superiority of the intellect can look for no linear route of escape from the dilemma. It cannot be otherwise, because such a person would have once again to apply the powers of the intellect. The only way out lies in a far-reaching change which is symbolized by being "drowned in the depths of the sea." The water of the sea stands for the world of our emotions, into which we should dive to balance the dominance of the intellect.

Somewhat further along in the same text we again come upon a saying about the pre-eminent significance of the soul which has been subjected to a rational diversion of its meaning. In verse 10 Jesus says, "See that you never despise any of these little ones, for I tell you that their angels in heaven are continually in the presence of my Father in heaven."

It sounds as if Jesus is giving away a secret, telling us that the angels of children stand nearer to God than do those of adults. But are we not grown-up children? Where lies the difference between us, and who sets the age limit? Obviously, this is an intellectual trick which clouds the message of the parable.

In line with our previous reflections, the translation of the words, "Their angels in heaven are continually in the presence of my Father in heaven," could mean in non-rational, sense-oriented language that Jesus wished to refer to the relationship with one's own soul on an especially high spiritual dimension. If the child stands for the forces of the human soul, then the angel of the child would symbolize its spiritual self, that is the divine core of a person's being. Through the eyes of the spiritual self, we are continually in the presence of the heavenly Father, because the core of our soul is one with his Being — provided, of course, that we understand the concept of the heavenly Father to be a synonym for the Godhead.

Logion 22 of the Gospel of Thomas makes it obvious that, in the sayings of Jesus, the concept of the child is meant symbolically and not concretely. This text has not been subjected to the process of revision which has affected the words of Jesus in the canonical gospels. This passage tells that Jesus saw some little children who were being fed at the breast and thereupon told his disciples, "These infants being suckled are like those who enter the Kingdom." The disciples misunderstood him, so they asked him, "Shall we then, as children, enter the Kingdom?" Jesus rejected this misunderstanding while elevating the symbolic value of his saying, as follows: "When you make the two one, and when you make the inside like the outside and the outside like the inside, and the above like the below... then you will enter (the Kingdom)."

It is clear from these words that in the parable of the child Jesus does not intend that people should become childishly naïve, that is, intellectually poor. Not in the least! What is intended is that we should overcome the superiority of the intellect, not through a suppression of the powers of understanding — they are an integral part of our individuality and a guarantee of our freedom — but through the awakening of a power in human beings which takes precedence — the power of love.

In the sayings of Jesus quoted above, love is presented as a power beyond logic, one with the ability to join together what rationally cannot be joined. How can we "make the two one" or the inner like the outer? It is only possible through a loving attitude towards whatever we encounter in life.

Through a loving attitude springing from the spiritual soul of the human being, it is possible to bridge the outward divisions and dismemberment of our world and, nestled in the all-encompassing Wholeness, experience within the harmony of its Being every situation which life brings. If a person persistently remains in such a loving condition and also has the courage to show it outwardly, then artificially erected boundaries and intellectual reservations dissolve in face of the Wholeness. Life is returned to the condition which Jesus described as the "kingdom of heaven."

When living in this condition, it is still perfectly possible to discriminate, make rational arrangements and decisions without harming the Wholeness, that is to say, the way in which all things belong together. The mind which beforehand stood in the service of division now becomes a tool of clarity for dealing creatively with life. Expressed symbolically, this means being the child and at the same time thinking and acting as the adult.

Chapter 8

Obstructive Patterns of Power

The reunion of the spiritual-soul extensions of my being
and consequent liberation of my inner voice, described in
the last chapter, finally enabled me to come to grips with a
part of the gospels which I had hitherto avoided. This concerned the complex of sayings which center on the 'unfruitful fig tree'. In my earlier preparations for this book I had
already felt that this embodied a pattern alien to the teaching of Jesus. However, I could not recognize its logic. The
story tells of an incident which is supposed to have happened to Jesus on the way to Jerusalem. It is reported in
Matthew as well as in Mark; I have chosen the latter version
because its description is more complete. "Next day as they
were leaving Bethany, he felt hungry. Seeing a fig tree in leaf
some distance away, he went to see if he could find any fruit
on it, but when he came up to it he found nothing but
leaves; for it was not the season for figs. And he addressed
the fig tree, 'May no one ever eat fruit from you again."
(Mark 11:12). "Next morning, as they passed by, they saw
the fig tree withered to the roots." (Mark 11:20)

My original reservations regarding the authenticity of
the story were based on the fact that I could not imagine
that Jesus would curse a living tree. I further asked myself
how he could condemn a fig tree for having no fruit when
— as the text expressly emphasizes — it was not yet time
for the fig harvest.

It is worth remembering that from time immemorial the
fig tree has been a symbol of the Mother Goddess. It is

capable of making unimaginably long roots and so can bring its luxuriant form to brighten places which are afflicted by drought and poor in vegetation. Thus, the fig tree is elevated to be the symbol of the unconquerable life forces of Mother Earth. Add to this that figs are exceptionally sweet and full of seeds, and it can be seen that the fig is also valued as a symbol of the inexhaustible fruitfulness of the Goddess.

The lofty symbolic meaning attached to the fig tree makes it clear that Jesus' curse struck a blow at the center of man's elementary trust in the wisdom of earth's systems, and therefore in the fruitfulness of the Earth Mother. In addition, the act of cursing was directly coupled with belief in God for the story continues: "Peter remembered. 'Look, Rabbi,' he said to Jesus, 'the fig tree that you cursed has withered away.' Jesus answered, 'Have faith in God. In truth I tell you, if anyone says to this mountain, "Be pulled up and thrown into the sea," with no doubt in his heart, but believing what he says will happen, it will be done for him.'" (Mark 11:23).

The danger in these words is that they can be understood to mean that Jesus was suggesting that people can do as they will with the planet, because he, Jesus, has cursed the power of the Earth Mother, which is to say, crippled it. The only condition attached which must be obeyed is belief in God.

When I began to see what a contorted pattern lay behind the complex of sayings about the cursing of the fig tree, I wished to come at its original source and started on various methods of investigation. By touching into the etheric layers of the relevant section of text, I found that it was put together from various parts. One of these parts, the statement about believing in one's heart, displayed a perfectly healthy etheric fabric, but others, such as the story of the actual cursing of the fig tree, had an etheric body which was alien to the teaching of Jesus. I see there an inner pic-

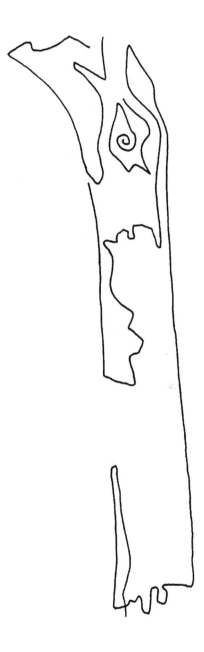

ture which characterizes the whole story. At the beginning there is a picture of a paradisiacally beautiful, luxuriant landscape. As soon as the tale reaches the scene of the curse, a dramatic reversal occurs: the living landscape collapses and there follows the picture of a completely dried and wasted country. As a third test, I took the complex of sayings into my heart and listened to the commentary of my inner voice. The answer, which I received from my heart center and wrote down at the same time, ran as follows: "Here you have stumbled on a poison. Without attracting anybody's notice, it was poured secretly into the inner layers of the gospel text to divert people's attention from the etheric message through which Jesus wished to reach his contemporaries' subconscious. They were not yet ready for the conscious understanding of his message of universal love."

At this point my feelings were allowed to sense the power of the poison. I felt a concentrated pain, as if I was having a heart attack. The inner voice continued, "It hurts. The poison of the false message has crippled the true one. It silenced the voice of the Mother of Life in the gospels. The voice of the Father of Light became over-powerful. In this way the balance of the Christian message was destroyed."

I was further referred to the danger which resides in coupling the curse on the fig tree with the statement about the power of belief and the ability to overthrow mountains. There arises from this a power triangle which conspicuously resembles the general impediments which divide the people of today from the Being of Earth and Nature. In respect of the statements about the fig tree complex, the three cornerstones of this barricade can be named as follows:

1. The voice of Mother Earth, which from time immemorial had led humanity through earthly life, is silenced for ever. (Key sentence: "May no one ever eat fruit from you again.")

2. People's inner heart-relationship with Earth and Nature is replaced by belief in a power which stands outside of humanity. (Key sentence: "Have faith in God.")
3. Humanity is promised dominion over the forces of Earth and Nature. (Key sentence: "If anyone says to this mountain, 'Be pulled up and thrown into the sea... it will be done for him.'")

The conjunction of these three elements awakens the impression of a person's omnipotence if they believe in a power which stands above them and gives them authority to do whatever they will. At the same time it releases them from responsibility to Mother Earth because it lets them believe that the wisdom and power of Earth are for naught. A human being can now overthrow mountains with a clear conscience, if he or she wishes.

I do not wish to place on the gospel texts alone the guilt for the manifold misunderstandings which have arisen among present-day people in regard to Earth and Nature. I am even convinced that it is not really a mistake, and consequently not a matter for guilt either.

Humanity's release from its symbiotic relationship with the wisdom of Earth and Nature was, at a certain point in history, unavoidable. This was so that a new, more far-reaching relationship with earth's systems could develop. For this reason, destructive processes were unleashed to free us from outdated ties. The unhappy story of the accursed fig tree belongs in this context.

It hurts me to trace the dark forces that have worked here subliminally. On the other hand, there is also reason to rejoice if the loss of the old, intimate relationship with Mother Earth enables our culture to discover a new love for the wisdom of Earth and Nature — called Sophia in Greek — and to anchor it in our consciousness deeper and more comprehensively than ever before.

Despite this conciliatory attitude, I feel that we are urgently commanded to make ourselves consciously aware of the force pattern which, as the above example shows, has caused our culture to look negatively on Earth and Nature. Only thus can its inhibiting power be recognized and consciously dismantled. The way will then be clear to build a new relationship with the Wisdom of Earth.

It is my feeling that I can best deprive this force-pattern of its obstructive power if I accept that, within the complex of the curse on the fig tree, there is some relationship to authentic sayings of Jesus which were joined together to form a rational statement. One of these sayings is the parable of the unfruitful fig tree mentioned in Luke. It contains a warning for humanity and may possibly have served as a model for the invention of the story of the curse on the fig tree. Jesus told the parable in the following way: "A man had a fig tree planted in his vineyard, and he came looking for fruit on it but found none. He said to his vinedresser, 'For three years now I have been coming to look for fruit on this fig tree and finding none. Cut it down: why should it be taking up the ground?' 'Sir,' the man replied, 'leave it one more year and give me time to dig round it and manure it: it may bear fruit next year; if not, then you can cut it down.'" (Luke 13:6).

Translated into logical language, the message of the parable runs something like this. Life is very kindly disposed to the human being's development. He or she is offered all possible ways, one after another, to take the next step on their personal path. But people are sluggish, we are afraid of changes and we hesitate. Life offers another chance, is patient and offers yet a further one. However, at a certain point in time it is no longer sensible to put off a decision. The flow of forces is hindered, and they accumulate. In one moment, completely unexpectedly, the inner tension builds up and the powers of change invade. A 'misfortune' strikes the dammed-up forces, and completely new circumstances are created. This is not about guilt and punishment, but about helping people onto a higher plane,

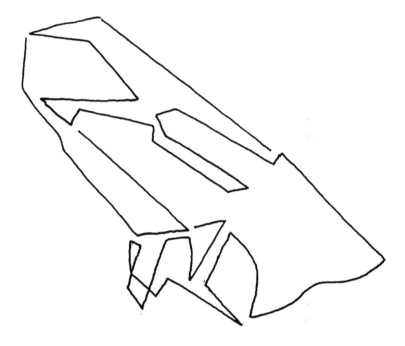

which our further evolution demands. On this account it was said: "It may bear fruit next year; if not, then you can cut it down."

Another of Jesus' sayings is also worked into the story of the curse. I sense this one to be completely credible. In order to understand its true message, I quote it here once again. "If anyone says to this mountain, 'Be pulled up and thrown into the sea,' with no doubt in his heart, but believing that what he says will happen, it will be done for him." (Mark 11:23).

It is significant that here the concept of belief is not bound up with an outside power which grants what a person wants, if only they believe in it strongly enough; on the contrary, the capacity for belief is referred to the indwelling power of the heart which participates in the divine source through the soul. A person is challenged to consciously lay aside their doubt and believe wholeheartedly in the perfection of life. If they succeed in believing instead of merely making an intellectual effort to believe, then, symbolically speaking, they can 'overthrow mountains'.

Outside the complex of the curse on the fig tree, I have discovered a second obstructive pattern of power in the gospel texts. I refer to a disastrous message in Matthew's gospel which I have already addressed several times. It concerns the division of people into 'good' and 'bad'; God is well disposed towards the first, and God damns the latter. The 'good' are praised and live in the promise of eternal happiness, whilst outermost darkness 'threatens' the 'bad'; "where there will be weeping and grinding of teeth." (Mat 25:30). This fear-inspiring refrain, which assures us that the bad will be "cast out" or "burnt", followed by "weeping and grinding of teeth," is systematically distributed through the whole of Matthew's text. This creates a regular pattern or network which subliminally impresses itself on the whole gospel message.

On the one hand, the complex of the curse on the fig

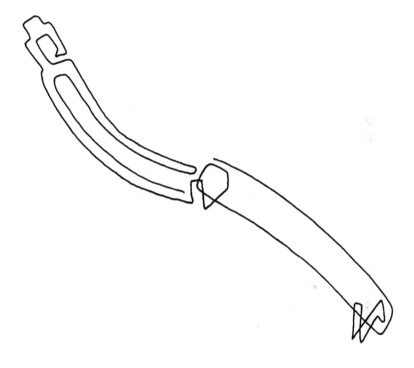

tree contains a hidden statement which works on the mental plane. On the other hand, the pattern of dividing people into good and bad works on the emotional plane. Feelings of fear are engendered, because one is uncertain to which of the two groups one belongs. A decision on the matter, so it is suggested, can be overturned at any moment, because the ethical and moral criteria for judging it are not clearly defined. Thus a person is constantly made to feel insecure and, with their fears secretly stirred, is reduced to psychic feebleness. Taken together, all the factors lead to guilt feelings and finally to a magnification of the original fear. The human being moves in a psychic vicious circle.

When, in the course of studying the etheric layers of the text, I discovered this disastrous power pattern, I was extremely angry. However, when I considered the composition of the gospels as a whole, I had to admit that this attempt at psychic brutality had its place and mission within the whole Christian tradition. Not only did the message of the parable of the tares (see Chapter 2) move me to this recognition, but also the role of Judas Iscariot within the circle of the apostles.

To assure the continuation of his work in Palestine, and later worldwide, Jesus chose a circle of twelve men who are called the apostles. Among them from the beginning was a man, Judas by name, who was to betray Jesus and deliver him to his crucifixion. So the four canonical gospels tell it. Jesus indicated many times that he knew the role that Judas would play. However, he never tried to unmask him or to exclude him from the circle of the chosen. According to John, when Jesus sat at table with his disciples during the last supper, he even said, "What you are going to do, do quickly." After Judas had departed from the circle, the role of traitor, interestingly enough, was taken over — though indignantly— by the outspoken, true-believing apostle Peter. In the further course of the Passion story, Peter three times denied his connection with Christ. I see this as an indication that what we are dealing with here is an objective role which appertains to every evolving person in the human community, and is not a subjective wickedness on the part of Judas Iscariot.

So that a person can develop as a free being — to address this theme once again — multiple possibilities are necessary. One must be able to choose independently among them, in order to learn to decide between those which encourage the unfolding of life and those which obstruct life's forces and lead to temptation. A person cannot possess these qualities without having first gone through difficult, disturbing or even destructive experiences. In this sense, one could even be inclined to accept the pattern of division as an element of challenge and testing within the evolution of the Christian culture.

However, a crystal clear dream demanded that I set some limits on my tolerance in this respect. On September 25, 1996, while staying in Berlin, I dreamed that something decisive was happening around me, though I did not notice how serious the situation was. The dream pictures left behind a clear feeling that they contained a warning.

The situation presented by the dream was as follows: there was a portion of humanity which was quite useless, and these people had voluntarily declared themselves ready to go to their death. I was present at the occasion of their destruction and could observe everything. Three people at a time were seated on a simple wooden bench and together lifted up and somehow toppled in nothingness. One could not see exactly what happened to them in this last phase. So far as I was concerned, the process was correct and natural. Although my beloved wife was also standing among those who awaited destruction, I did not feel that the situation was so serious that I could not leave right away and go about my business.

In the next instant I became conscious of the fateful

nature of the situation; I turned around, ran back into the room, beckoned violently and shouted that I wished to say goodbye to my wife. She was already sitting on the wooden bench, so the process of destruction was delayed. While, still rather indifferent, I was going towards her, one of the participants remarked mockingly, "Look, Marika is going to get another little kiss!"

At that moment there was a cry from the furthest corner of the room. A woman's voice cried out, "Paper, paper!" I looked around and saw a woman in the distance beckoning with a sheet of paper. Everything was happening at lightning speed. My intuition told me something like, "Free speech is now here." At once I began to shout with all my might, "I do not allow it!" I put every ounce of decision behind these words, directed against the idea that people should be destroyed here as a matter of course.

The spiritual attitude expressed in my cold-blooded consent to the division of humanity into halves of 'good' and 'bad' lay deep in my subconscious, and the dream encouraged it to come to the light of day. The urgency running through the whole dream indicates how important it is for us to become aware right now of the destructive consequences of this black-and-white thinking. Humanity is at this moment struggling to recognize and organize itself as a manifold and yet unified planetary organism, but its efforts will be fundamentally weakened and hampered as long the old dualistic patterns remain in force.

It is not enough for us to support the human rights of every person on earth; nor is it enough for us to work for the just division of goods among all the inhabitants of the planet. The core of my dream message was that all these efforts would miss the goal if at the same time we did not work on our dawning consciousness of the outdated and obstructive power patterns which are impressed upon our culture at the levels of soul and spirit.

The division of mankind into two halves, of which one

— as indicated in the dream — is in danger of being excluded from our joint evolution, stands in glaring contradiction to the message of one of the 'Shepherds of Mankind', the angel Michael. He confirms beyond any doubt that everyone — that really means every individual person — has their immutable place in the entire composition of humanity. One of these messages, which my colleague Ana received on September 15, 1996, was quoted in Chapter 4. She wrote down a second one on September 22, 1996, three days before I had my dream more than a thousand kilometers away in Berlin. I will summarize the main points of Michael's message as follows:

• Every single person represents a unity, like a small stone in the mosaic comprising the entirety of humanity. Each unity has a significance for the whole which is of equal value, without consideration whether the person who represents this unity is more or less evolved.

• The individual person is a rounded and many layered unity which continually gathers experiences and information, digests them, passes them on and exchanges them with others. From this process there arises something which one can compare to a high voltage network on a superior plane, which binds the individual persons together.

• This network of relationships between people is worked out with unbelievable refinement and precision, so that in each moment an individual person can make exactly that contact and receive that information which is needed for their evolution.

• The quality of the exchange, and of all the relationships to which a person is attracted, depend on the evolutionary step on which they are standing; therefore, at any given moment their need may be for pleasant, unpleasant or challenging, experiences.

• No encounter is meaningless; every relationship into which a person enters carries within itself an experience which can lead to an understanding — depending on whether the person is conscious or unconscious of the exchange which is needed.

- It is therefore worth learning to look on every one of your fellow men and women as a junction point in a great network, and to understand that you yourself are just such a junction point.
- Thus we can view the world around us, and the many people who surround us, as a multi-dimensional organism through which all participants can gather knowledge and grow.
- For a person to be a creative member of this multiplicity, it is first necessary to listen within and, to a certain degree, get to know your own being. Only through this can a person be ready to exchange with the Wholeness.

I believe that I have found in the gospel texts sufficient evidence to show that Jesus himself taught the abolition of the Matthean dualism and that his general message was devoted to the integration of opposites and not to a division into black and white. There is a well known account of how he expressly refused to take over the role of a divider. The incident is recounted in the Gospel of Thomas as well as in Luke. Unfortunately, Luke puts it in a moralizing context (Luke 12:13), so that its original message is lost. I therefore quote from Thomas: "(A man said) to him, 'Tell my brothers to divide my father's possessions with me.' He said to him, 'O man, who has made me a divider?' He turned to his disciples and said to them, 'I am not a divider, am I?'" (Tm, Log. 72).

The author of Luke's gospel could find no rational sense in this saying. He has rearranged it so that it gives the impression that the man had been eager to obtain the goods of his dead father. This shifts the emphasis and in consequence, the incident leads into an obviously self-concocted saying which is put in Jesus' mouth: "Watch, and be on your guard against avarice of any kind." (Luke 12:15).

The message in Logion 61 is more productive. A trace of this saying, undoubtedly original, is also preserved in the canonical gospels of Luke and Matthew. Unfortunately, the words were used as a cornerstone to underpin a secondary content which was felt to be more important than the message itself. The secondary content concerns Jesus' revelations about the future. Thus that portion of Jesus' words which suited the new content were taken over into the text, and the others left out.

According to Thomas, the saying consists of three parts. The first part was taken over into the canonical gospels in a modified form: "Jesus said, 'Two will rest on a bed: the one will die, and the other will live." (Tm, Log. 61).

In Luke it says correspondingly, "I tell you, on that night, when two are in one bed, one will be taken, the other left; when two women are grinding corn together, one will be taken, the other left." (Luke 17:34).

When one views this passage apart from the whole saying, it awakens the impression that Jesus has spoken about the partition of humanity into two halves, of which one will be led forward into the future and the other abandoned to decay. This way of interpreting the text corresponds to the role assigned to the sayings about division in the context of the two canonical gospels. It serves to introduce the idea of a future 'Last Judgment', when 'the sheep' are allegedly to be parted from 'the goats', that is to say, the good people and the bad people separated for all eternity.

From the above, we get a general impression that the sayings of Jesus emphasize that the two people who experience the division lie in one and the same bed, grind at the same mill or — according to Matthew — are in the same field. This indicates that the sayings do not concern two different persons, but refer to two sides of one and the same person. Jesus is referring to an inner division within a person. This division is temporarily necessary for our inner development to be made possible. But there comes a point

in time when it must be overcome. In the process of unification, that side which has lived in blindness detaches itself. In the two sentences quoted above, Jesus wished to make us conscious of this complex connection.

According to the Gospel of Thomas, Jesus spoke these words while he sat at table with his hostess, a woman called Salome. At once Salome took notice and asked who he might be. Jesus answered, "I am He who exists from the Undivided. I was given some of the things of My father." When she heard this she replied, full of conviction, "I am Your disciple."

To overcome the inner division within the human being, Jesus brought into the world the teaching of the integrated human. People are inwardly split today in many aspects. On one side they participate in the material world, on the other they are sunk in a dream consciousness. When a person thinks of that side of themselves which they show in public, they think also of their quality as a private person, and so on. For people to experience healthy development, this sort of psychic-spiritual split must be eliminated. We have to decide which of the inwardly dwelling forces and qualities promote the future, and which hinder development.

In order to achieve unity in oneself — Jesus characterized himself as, "He who exists from the Undivided" — we must tread the way of change and take the path which cherishes and encourages those aspects which bear the future in themselves. The other aspects which lead to conflict, disunity, equivocation and doubt must be recognized, disempowered and excluded. In this sense we can understand the saying, "Two will rest on a bed: the one will die, and the other will live."

The importance of Jesus' teaching about the reunion of human beings is emphasized by the sentence, "I was given some of the things of My father." By this, Jesus wishes to tell us that this teaching was shared with him by the

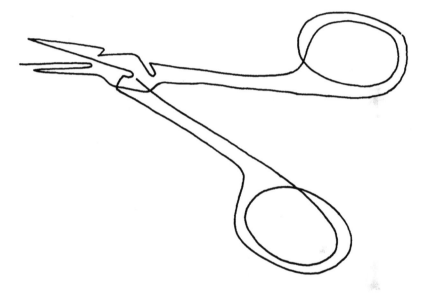

'Shepherds of Mankind', that is to say, by the highest principle to watch over and support our evolution.

To once again express its content in all clarity, Jesus adds,
"Therefore I say, if he is (undivided), he will be filled with
light, but if he is divided, he will be filled with darkness."
(Tm, Log. 61). Is anything more needed to recognize that
the power pattern dividing mankind into halves of good and
bad is conditioned by time, and today is outdated?

Chapter 9

The Several Layers
of Jesus' Teaching

Of all the parables handed down from Jesus, the parable of
the sower is surely the best known. All three synoptic
gospels are in basic agreement as to its form. The recent discovery of the Gospel of Thomas has brought still more con-
vincing confirmation of its authenticity. The gospels even
provide an interpretation attributed to Jesus himself. The
problem is that the message of the parable of the sower has
a many layered character, and the meaning which Jesus
entrusted to his disciples addresses only one of these layers
— illuminating it in the light of the teaching which he was
trying to impart to them.

Jesus had told his disciples to spread the words of the
gospel among the people and he interpreted the parable of
the sower for them in the sense of this commission, in such
a way that they should learn from it. However, this does not
mean that he would not have interpreted the parable in
another form for other groups of men and women. I would
like to make that much plain in advance before quoting the
parable, so as to ensure that the usual interpretation does
not disguise the several layers of the message, which actually deals with the several dimensions of life.

"A sower went out to sow his seed. Now as he sowed,
some fell on the edge of the path and was trampled on; and
the birds of the air ate it up. Some seed fell on rock, and

when it came up it withered away, having no moisture. Some seed fell in the middle of thorns and the thorns grew with it and choked it. And some seed fell into good soil and grew and produced its crop a hundredfold." (Luke 8:5).

Transposed into logical form, the parable's message means that humanity consists of four groups, each related to the evolutionary step which an individual's personal development has enabled them to reach. These groups are not divided from each other on planet Earth, such that one lives in the north, one in the south, another in the east and the fourth in the west, but each group is co-mingled with the others. In this way they remain in constant interaction, and this has the effect of encouraging the development of the whole human family. Based on the parable of the sower, one can define in the following way the four inter-penetrating layers from which humanity is put together:

1. To the first and most widespread layer belong the many individuals who are capable of consciousness but are 'asleep', meaning that they struggle with the circumstances of their daily lives and have not yet devoted themselves consciously to growth. Symbolically speaking, they have not yet made the effort to plow the field of their consciousness. Its surface is hard and compact, like that of a path. For this reason it is said, "Some fell on the edge of the path and was trampled on; and the birds of the air ate it up."

2. The second layer is composed of persons who occasionally interest themselves in healthy life forms, such as the development of individual soul capacities and certain spiritual ideals. They are happy to read reports about other people who have distinguished themselves on their paths of spiritual evolution, but do nothing to enter into the experience for themselves. ("Some seed fell on rock, and when it came up it withered away, having no moisture.")

3. To the third layer belong those personalities who are con-

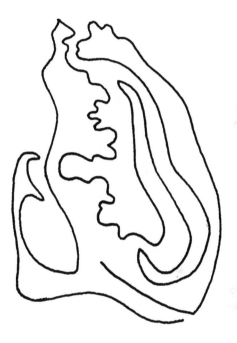

sciously ready to go on their evolutionary path. They are also inclined to be enthusiastic about specific spiritual streams, and may temporarily follow this or that teacher or guru, or practice a particular spiritual discipline. However, their efforts lack consistency or do not delve deep enough. They are distracted every time by the circumstances and pressures of external life, and their inner development is forgotten. ("Some seed fell in the middle of thorns and the thorns grew with it and choked it.")

4. Finally, within the human family there is a fourth layer which comprises relatively few individuals; they work consciously and persistently on their personal development and try to realize in their daily life what they have inwardly experienced and learnt. In the parable they are characterized by the sentence: "And some seed fell into good soil and grew and produced its crop a hundredfold."

The parable should in no way be understood in the manner it is usually interpreted, namely that Jesus reproached those who belonged to the first three groups and praised the fourth. All four groups are equally important if our evolution is to unfold as a whole, and each is necessary for the further development of the others. If it were not for the existence of the first, 'dullest,' group, the people of the second group would have nobody to tell of their enthusiasms, nobody for whom to write their novels, engage in politics, or build the economy... but when their creativity can help someone else's development advance, then they are themselves motivated to go further on their way, and so they grow. Similarly, speaking of the relationships between all four groups of people, one can say that they all mutually encourage each other and there is not one which is superfluous.

Jesus' message should not be understood as a one-dimensional teaching but as corresponding to these differences in people. Every time it is reduced to a single meaning is like a rape. The parable of the sower offers us an excellent key for interpreting the several dimensions of his works in Palestine at the beginning of our era. To put it briefly, Jesus taught on four different levels simultaneously to try to bring his message to all the people.

The first-named level of the human family, usually described as ' the masses', was called 'this generation' by Jesus. They are often mentioned in his sayings, for example in the words: "What comparison, then, can I find for the people of this generation? What are they like? They are like children shouting to one another while they sit in the marketplace: 'We played the pipes for you and you wouldn't dance; we sang dirges, and you wouldn't cry.'" (Luke 7:31). Life more or less passes them by, with all its wonderful but often challenging possibilities for inner growth.

The masses' relationship to Christ's message is differently expressed in a Logion from the Gospel of Thomas: "I took My place in the midst of the world, and I appeared to them in flesh. I found all of them intoxicated; I found none of them thirsty. And My soul became afflicted for the sons of men, because they are blind in their hearts and do not have sight; for empty they came into the world, and empty too they seek to leave the world. But for the moment they are intoxicated. When they shake off their wine, then they will repent." (Tm, Log. 28).

The last portion of the saying indicates that it was not Jesus' way to turn his back on the masses of humanity and do nothing to help them further on their way. But to achieve that without a meaningless waste of strength demands action of a special kind. Concerning this, Jesus speaks as follows: " It is an evil and unfaithful generation that asks for a sign! The only sign it will be given is the sign of the prophet Jonah. For as Jonah remained in the belly of the sea monster the three days and three nights, so will the Son of man be in the heart of the earth for three days and three nights." (Mat 12:39).

It is obvious that by the sign of Jonah he means his crucifixion. This, accompanied by the change in the interior of the earth and the resurrection from the dead which followed, was the most conspicuous of the public miracles which Jesus wrought. To these public acts also belong his miracles and deeds of healing. These latter were works which directly touched the souls of the people affected and were also means by which his message could reach the mass consciousness.

We can turn up our nose today and question the authenticity of the miracles and the reliability of the reports about them. The fact is however that a new religion was founded based on these signs and wonders. Corresponding to it was a social form which, above all, could help the people of the simplest of the four levels. I am thinking of the form of the Christian Church.

The second group of people are those persons who are interested in pursuing their development on the inner path. They are not however capable of doing this independently. In a conversation with his disciples Jesus has characterized them in the following way: "To you is granted to understand the secrets of the kingdom of God; for the rest it remains in parables, so that they may look but not perceive, listen but not understand." (Luke 8:10).

These are the people who felt attracted to Jesus through his teaching, and who very often gathered around him as he went from village to village and from town to town and gladly listened to him. He spoke to them in the coded speech of parables, whose message they could better accept through pictures, feelings and intuition. They certainly 'heard' the message but they could not understand it. In consequence, they were not capable of bringing it consciously into their daily life. But, from beyond the conscious plane, they could be brought onto the path.

The third group of people are represented in the gospel texts by the scribes and the strict Judaic sect of Pharisees. They are those who are trained in questions of the spiritual truths and laws, and on the basis of this training often occupy a corresponding public office and yet too often succumb to the temptations of ambition and wealth. The gospel texts are full of the criticisms which Jesus launched at them. Here are some examples:

- "Jesus said, 'The Pharisees and scribes have taken the keys of Knowledge and hidden them. They themselves have not entered, nor have they allowed to enter those who wish to.'" (Tm, Log. 39).
- "You Pharisees! You clean the outside of cup and plate, while inside yourselves you are filled with extortion and wickedness. Fools! Did not he who made the outside make the inside too?" (Luke 11:39).
- "You blind guides, straining out gnats and swallowing camels!" (Mat 23:24).

Finally we arrive at the fourth, most refined level of individuals, those of whom the parable of the sower says, "Some seed fell into good soil and grew and produced its crop a hundredfold." These are individuals who consciously strive to make their whole life into a spiritual path. Jesus spoke about them as follows: "Let him who seeks continue seeking until he finds. When he finds, he will become troubled. When he becomes troubled, he will be astonished, and he will rule over the All." (Tm, Log. 2).

These words make quite clear that the fourth and highest of the evolutionary steps is not only concerned with the acquisition of knowledge; rather, precedence is given to the processes of inner change which the seeker undergoes while pursuing it. It begins with the disruption and collapse of the old patterns of belief and action. The process leads further to an awe of what is new and so far unknown and is now being shared with humans, and it finds its longed-for consummation when it anchors itself in the eternal core of Being. Such a one will 'rule over the All.'

However, we should not think that humanity's highest developed level is in any way uniform. When people have reached the step where they begin to independently seek their way to knowledge, life branches out into a rich variety of options. There is a new sort of diversity occurring which belongs to another level of potency. As seekers, we stand on various steps of personal development.

There are those who have outgrown their inner insecurities and fears and consequently can move relatively effortlessly over the waves of life without having to battle with soul-searching problems. And there are others who must go through personal trials or humiliating circumstances in order to have the experiences which will help them proceed further on their way.

Jesus' parable of the workers in the vineyard, given us in the Gospel according to Matthew, assures us that the divine pattern of life is fair for everyone. However, since we have been presented with the gift of free will, we are responsible for the road which we choose to take in order to realize this pattern. In the end it depends on us how long we suffer, or enjoy ourselves, on the road.

"Now the kingdom of Heaven is like a landowner going out at daybreak to hire workers for his vineyard. He made an agreement with the workers for one denarius a day and sent them to his vineyard. Going out at about the third hour he saw others standing idle in the market place and said to them, 'You go to my vineyard too and I will give you a fair wage.' So they went. At about the six hour and again at about the ninth hour, he went out and did the same. Then at about the eleventh hour he went out and found more men standing around, and he said to them, 'Why have you been standing here idle all day?' 'Because no one has hired us,' they answered. He said to them, 'You go into my vineyard too.' In the evening, the owner of the vineyard said to his bailiff, 'Call the workers and pay them their wages, starting with the last arrivals and ending with the first.' So those who were hired at about the eleventh hour came forward and received one denarius each. When the first came, they expected to get more, but they too received one denarius each. They took it, but grumbled at the landowner saying, 'The men who came last have done only one hour, and you have treated them the same as us, though we have done a heavy day's work in all the heat.' He answered one of them and said, 'My friend, I am not being unjust to you; did we not agree on one denarius? Take your earnings and go. I choose to pay the lastcomer as much as I pay you.'" (Mat 20).

If we stubbornly persist in denying our true self and suppressing our life's many layers, we will be led through difficulties which sooner or later will open our eyes. On the other hand, if we pay attention to the pieces of knowledge which come towards us and give ourselves over to the changes which our life brings with it, our path will be easy and happy.

For this reason it is unwise to make the landowner who hires workers for different hours for identical wages' responsible for our misfortune. Instead, it is worth making the effort to complete the necessary changes so as to be able also to reach the step where a person can enjoy life wholeheartedly.

The parable of the sower gives us a good understanding of the several layered nature of humanity, and also of the several corresponding layers in the message which Jesus has given us. But the Being of the individual person is also organized in several layers or dimensions. The person of Jesus, as he is mediated to us through the gospels, stands as a model for the several dimensions of the Being of men and women. In his life, Jesus preceded us in these dimensions, so that it would be easier for us, in the following generations, to recognize the several dimensions in ourselves and realize them in our personal life.

First, we should examine the reports of the personality of Jesus which was rooted in the time, place and social norms of his epoch. This layer of his Being is brought to our consciousness through a question posed by his neighbors in Nazareth: "Where did the man get this wisdom and these miraculous powers? This is the carpenter's son, surely? Is not his mother the woman called Mary, and his brothers James and Joseph and Simon and Jude? His sisters, too, are they not all here with us?" (Mat 13:54). Jesus severely criticized this way of looking at people, which does not recognize the human individuality in its several layers but tries to reduce it to its mere external appearance. He did this to make his contemporaries, who thought and lived like this, conscious of their one-sided view. The following is a typical event from his life: "His mother and his brothers came looking for him, but they could not get to him because of the crowd. He was told, 'Your mother and brothers are standing outside and want to see you.' But he said in answer, 'My mother and my brothers are those who hear the word of God and put it into practice.'" (Luke 8:19).

Jesus is not denying that everyday life is important for the development of a person's being, but rather is refusing to countenance a one-dimensional relationship to life, one which would suppress its variety. His was an attitude of critical warning in the face of a one-sided, linear concentration on the fabric of life. This is made clear in the parable of a rich man, reported by several gospels: "There was a rich man who had much money. He said, 'I shall put my money to use so that I may sow, reap, plant, and fill my storehouse with produce, with the result that I shall lack nothing. Such were his intentions, but that same night he died. Let him who has ears hear." (Tm, Log. 63).

Beyond that part of the personality of Jesus which is rooted in space and time and in its life's course limited between birth and death, the gospels reveal two further dimensions of his Being. In this sense the most informative is the passage where Jesus asks his disciples who they think he is. There are four reports of this definitive conversation, three in the canonical gospels and a further one in the recently discovered Gospel of Thomas. Outwardly it may appear as if, in their uniformity, the first three diverge from the fourth. The truth, however, is that all four present the individuality of Jesus as threefold. In Logion 13 of the Gospel of Thomas, the threefold organization of Jesus' Being is given the following form:

1. "You are like a wise philosopher."
2. "You are like a righteous angel."
3. "Master, my mouth is totally incapable of saying whom You are like."

The earthly plane of the being of man is named first (1). This is tied to the requirements of earth's systems and must go through the changes of birth and death in order to take part in earthly life. Quite different is the second plane of our being which exists from eternity to eternity (2). This is the plane of our soul which has a spiritual-energetic form, and in its consciousness can be compared to an angel. To these is now added the divine core of man (3), which is so all-embracing in its Being that it cannot adequately be expressed; on this account it is said: "Master, my mouth is totally incapable of saying whom You are like."

We discussed in Chapter 6 how through his presence Jesus preceded the human being of today, which is now realizing itself but then was still in the future, and we can therefore see how the threefold organization of Jesus' Being is a model for ourselves. Following the Logion quoted above, we can name the three aspects of the human being as follows:

1. The earthly aspect of the human being.
2. The angelic soul of the human being.
3. The divine core of the human being.

In the canonical gospels the same conversation is worded in such a way that the three aspects of Jesus' being are masked in biblical symbols. However, the basic structure outlined above is still recognizable:

1. Some believe Jesus to be John the Baptist, who is

esteemed as a pious and holy man.
2. Some believe Jesus to be Elijah or another prophet.
   Since the role of a prophet is to bring a divine message to
   man, it is comparable to the role of angels who serve as
   messengers between the spiritual and the manifested
   worlds.
3. "Peter spoke up and said to him, 'You are the Christ.'"
   (Mark 8:29). (The Christ means "the Anointed of God").

However, I refuse to equate these three layers of the
human being with the customary idea of a trinity of body,
soul and spirit, because in the last analysis this concept conveys a hierarchical arrangement which looks on the body as
the lowest and the spirit as the highest aspect of our identity. On the contrary, my experience suggests that the earthly plane of the human being is not only a body which bears
the soul, but is a consummate creation of earth's systems, as
perfect as a mountain, river or tree. Certainly, as such it has
no individual existence, because it is part of the whole
Being of Earth, just as are the tree, the river or the mountain. On the other hand, the earthly plane of the human
being possesses a perfect, vital-energetic organism, consummate in itself; and also an unlimited intelligence in which
all the creatures of earth partake — and not just those with
materialized bodies. In this sense the saying in Logion 63
can be understood: "You are like a wise philosopher."

Furthermore, the third, divine aspect of the human
being is not that part of our identity which simply super-
vises the other two, in hierarchical fashion. Rather, these
two other aspects, the 'earthly human' and the 'soul
human', are interpenetrated and borne up by the divine
presence. In no way does the Higher Self hover over them
like a cloud. The divine spirit penetrates us as much from
the cosmic as from the earthly side, as Jesus understood and
expressed very clearly when he identified himself with the
divine aspect of his Being: " It is I who am the All. From
Me did the All come forth, and unto Me did the All extend.

Split a piece of wood, and I am there. Lift up the stone, and you will find Me there." (Tm, Log. 77). The divine presence in man is here confirmed as much in its universal as in its earthly aspect.

The soul is that aspect which mediates between the divine core of the human being and our earthly form. A message from the angel Michael, which has as its theme the several dimensions of life, describes in the following way the role of the soul in a person's life:

• For some time before conception the soul busies itself with preparations for the human's earthly path; after death it finally rises slowly from the body.

• The soul is not bound up with time. It exists both before and after.

• In contrast to the earthly aspect, it represents the human's spiritual aspect. Its role is to lead him or her through life.

• It leads the human into various experiences and so allows necessary pieces of information to flow in from past lives.

• The soul maintains the holistic pattern of the individual's development and by imparting impulses is able to lead the human being to their goal.

In the Gospel of Thomas the universal quality of a person's soul is outlined in the following terms: "Jesus said, 'If they say to you, 'Where did you come from?', say to them, 'We came from the light, the place where the light came into being on its own accord and established (itself) and became manifest through their image.' If they say to you, 'Is it you?', say, 'We are its children, and we are the elect of the Living Father.' If they ask you, 'What is the sign of your Father in you?', say to them, 'It is movement and repose.'''' (Tm, Log.50)

It is especially noteworthy that in this saying a paradox is chosen to be the sign of our divine core — presented here as 'the Father'. How should something which rests in perfect peace also be able to move with the speed of light? In our world this is impossible because it is illogical; however in the dimension from which the soul arises such a contradiction is reality. It is even a characteristic feature of the nature of the soul, which lies beyond linear logic. The human as an incarnated being, the human as a light form, and the human as a revelation of the divine, original Being, these are three dimensions of our identity. Jesus has lived them before us as the archetype, so that the people of succeeding generations may have a model to follow for their further development.

Chapter 10

Who Jesus Was
and Who Christ Is

It is unfortunate that the many dimensions of Jesus' person were too often forgotten in the process of consolidating and interpreting the gospel texts. In fact, there was an attempt to reduce his being to a single dimension. Even while the divine aspect of Jesus was being emphasized and trumpeted abroad, the all-embracing nature of his works and teaching for Mankind was down-played.

The effort to limit Jesus to a single denominator and to present this viewpoint as the only possible one may be illustrated by two examples which have different points of emphasis. One comes from the orthodox Gospel according to Matthew, the other from the Gospel of Thomas, which in places is colored by Gnosticism.

In Matthew there was an attempt to establish and reinforce the institutionalization of the Christian message; in Thomas the impulse was to nurture an esoteric variant. Both efforts made reference to one and the same event in Jesus' life: the conversation, already mentioned, between the Master and his disciples in which he asks them about his person.

In Matthew's Gospel (however not in Mark or Luke where the same conversation also occurs), Peter's answer to Jesus' question, who he might be, is celebrated as the only correct one. It reads: "You are the Christ, the Son of the living God." (Mat 16:16). Based on this reply, we have the proclamation of the foundation of the future ecclesiastical community and its later institutionalization: "Jesus replied, 'Simon son of Jonah, you are a blessed man! Because it was no human agency that revealed this to you but my Father in heaven. So I now say to you: You are Peter[1] and on this rock I will build my community. And the gates of the underworld can never overpower it. I will give you the keys of the kingdom of Heaven: whatever you bind on earth will be bound in heaven; whatever you loose on earth will be loosed in heaven.'" (Mat 16:17).

Here we have an image of people's future connection to the message of Christ, one which rests on the principle of a community under patriarchal leadership. It strongly supports the principle that people should be influenced from without.

On the other hand, the variant of the same conversation between Jesus and his disciples, as it is written down in the Gospel of Thomas, offers an entirely contrary vision. This however is just as one-dimensional as the first. There it says that after Thomas answered the question, who Jesus might be, with the words, "Master, my mouth is wholly incapable of saying whom You are like," Jesus took him on one side and revealed to him three secret sayings which he did not entrust to the other apostles. Thomas rebuffed their insistent questions in a manner which was bound to greatly exaggerate the significance of the secret contained in the three sayings. "Thomas said to them, 'If I tell you one of the things which he told me, you will pick up stones and throw them at me; a fire will come out of the stones and burn you up.'" (Tm, Log. 13).

In this case, the image of people's future connection with the message which Jesus brought into the world is

---

1 Petros means 'rock' in Greek and is the name which Jesus gave to his apostle Simon.

grounded in a transcendental secret. Instead of following the confession of faith and other prescriptions by which the Church binds its members, individuals are here challenged to commit themselves to search for enlightenment on their own and along an uncertain path. The three secret sayings stand for the key which can open the gates of ultimate knowledge. Is this the same key which, in the orthodox version, was pressed into Peter's hand?

These are attempts, in one way or another, to rip Jesus' person out of the fabric of life and glorify him. I should like to compare them with my own personal experience of his presence. This goes back to my memory of a life when I was a contemporary of Jesus in Palestine.

To introduce this account, I have to say that during the last few years, ever since my sensitivity increased noticeably, I have made an interesting observation. Every time I mentioned Jesus and his teachings in my discussions, people suddenly sat up and took notice. It felt as though the listeners — doubtless unconsciously — were perceiving that my words were based on some experience which made them credible. For myself however, this background experience was then still unknown to me: I could only wonder at what was going on.

I presumed to make my first attempt to follow up on this mystery during my retreat in September 1997, which was also when I gained access to the inner voice. I had the feeling that my investigations in this direction must be safeguarded by sufficient objectivity.

When I concentrated on my heart center and asked about the origin of the above-mentioned experience, my attention was drawn down into the great sea of the subconscious. Then, certain feelings and vibrational patterns began to rise up into my consciousness. These took on specific forms of expression which were comprehensible logically and as pictures. I immediately began to write them down.

My first contact with the presence of Jesus was not an actual meeting. I was a young man and was walking through the narrow lanes of our village. On the corner of a side-alley I saw a group of villagers standing, among whom was a woman speaking loudly about some event. I was magnetically attracted to her voice, and stood by and listened. The talk was all about a man who habitually behaved as if he were one of the old prophets returned to life. What most impressed me was the fact that at one point the woman broke out in weeping because she was so overcome by her memory of the truth of his words. One could understand nothing more of what she was saying. I went on my way much moved.

Her experience had shaken me to my depths and put me in some confusion. I suspected that something was happening which would cause me to question my convictions. I had long thought to prepare myself for a life such as my forebears had lived. I saw myself only as a member of a long, previously defined, generational chain. Now I felt that I was confronting a surprising change which would tear me away from this chain.

The second meeting with Jesus' presence happened in a neighboring town. The news reached our village that the prophet was staying there for a while, teaching and healing. I knew at once that I must go there. I hurried off, ran along the familiar paths leading down from the arid hill and reached the town at evening. I asked for directions and was sent to one of the more distinguished houses. There I found a circle of people closely gathered around the light of an oil lamp. A man was sitting and talking among them. He spoke in an exceptionally calm voice and I was astonished at its effect on the crowd of listeners. I joined the circle and listened with every part of my being. I could understand nothing, all was new to me. I felt however that the man was speaking the truth and that through his words there flowed a love which touched the deepest layers of my being.

The hour was already late by the time the circle silently dispersed, and the host invited me to spend the remainder of the night in a corner of the room. There I slept curled up, covered by a hairshirt. In the night I dreamed that I was still a young teenager and that the stranger who had bewitched me with his words was leading me to the edge of a precipice. With his hand he pointed to the valley beneath us. To look at, it was paradisiacally beautiful, bathed in the light of all the colors of the rainbow. Still dreaming, I felt that my life's purpose would be to find this valley.

While those memories rose up out of the storehouse of my subconscious, parallel associations came to me. These showed how much the pattern of my present life is built on the foundations then laid in Palestine. For example, the above-mentioned dream has also come to me at another of my life's turning points. This was on December 24, 1980, when I was facing a decision about making changes in my life and devoting my artwork to a deeper relationship with Earth and her healing.

Then too I stood on the edge of a wonderfully beautiful valley and was considering whether I would not rather fly over it instead of committing myself to go down and put myself in its power. Now I understood. This wonderful valley, thrust into the center of my consciousness, symbolized then and now that quality of life which Jesus called the kingdom of heaven. It is no small challenge, to seek this quality in life and bring it home to the consciousness of one's fellow men.

My third memory of meeting with the presence of Jesus was in Jerusalem. I was going down a bustling street — it was teeming with people and animals and thronged with vendors' stalls — when I saw Jesus coming towards me with a group of his disciples. Making up my mind on the spur of the moment, I pressed towards him through the crowd and asked to be allowed to be his disciple. His reaction puzzled me: instead of embracing me, he took a step backward as if he wanted to look through me from head to toe. Then he said to me, "Go, my son, and become who you are."

I was shocked. I had imagined that he would be seeking like-minded people and rejoice in my decision. Instead, he turned me away. In the meantime he had disappeared with his disciples into the crowd, while I stood there still rooted to the spot. My fear was that I was not good enough to be his pupil. Yet at the same time I had a feeling which gave me courage. Something in me suspected that the words the Master had spoken came from an insight into the secret of my soul.

It seemed then as if I did not meet Jesus again after that incident in Jerusalem, nor did I seek for him. It was not that I was offended. Rather, I had the feeling that his dismissal had a deeper reason which I still could not understand. Ever and again I turned over in my memory the words which he had spoken me in Jerusalem. When he had said, "Go and be who you are," could he have meant that he was sending me back to my everyday life? But he had said, "Become who you are..."

At that point I expected to derive no more useful information and wanted to cease from my delving in the storehouse of memory. Then like a geyser, high out of the depths, there shot a memory which obviously had no wish to be overlooked: I had come in contact with Jesus once more, though not directly, during that time in Palestine.

I was present in Jerusalem during that Passover Festival when Jesus was crucified. I can remember the atmosphere in the city, a mixture of anxious fear, uncertainty and oppression. Because I respected the Master's wish for me to keep my distance, I did not try to approach his circle. Everything which I experienced of this event, I had from street conversations and the feelings which these aroused in me. When I heard talk that he was to be crucified, I believed that the affair concerned some conflict between him and the priesthood, which had come to a dramatic head but would soon blow over. When later the news reached me that he was really on the way to his crucifixion, I was puzzled. Waves of doubt flooded over me. If he was really a messenger of God, would he not have possessed the wisdom to have avoided crucifixion?

I felt as if psychologically overtaxed by this situation which had turned into a crucifixion. I began to wander through the city and search for anybody who could give me an explanation.

On my way I saw a woman whom I knew belonged to the circle close to Jesus. I marveled that she was going peacefully through the city while something frightful was facing her teacher. She looked me in the eyes and said in a calm voice, "What you hear spoken of is only the outward side of something which at its core is wonderful. It will open the gate into the future for us." Then she went silently on her way.

Once again I experienced what had already happened twice before in my encounters with Jesus: the world turning over and putting me upside down. Scarcely had I accustomed myself to his revolutionary teaching and begun to carry it over into my life — for many of my contemporaries around me spoke of his sayings while I listened — than I now stumbled over a new mystery. I felt that it gave my life a much wider framework — today I would describe it as the process of human evolution. Then however, I had still no idea how to give a name to such a mystery. And yet after this brief meeting a quiet peace came over me, and I knew that, despite the fearful nature of the event, all would be well.

I think that my memories of the presence of Jesus, even though mediated through the experience of one who was on the edge of the events, are sufficient evidence to contradict the glamour which has later enveloped him. In my memory there is an unmistakable sense of his grounded and modest way of behaving. This corresponds with his own efforts to evade the desires and attempts of his contemporaries to declare him the Chosen One of God. In several places the gospels report how he forbade those who recognized his divine origin to speak of it. Also, in Mark and Luke, the report of Jesus' question, who he might be, does not close with the appointment of the disciple Peter to be head of the future Church, but with a simple prohibition to speak publicly about his role as Christ.

And yet my memory of those experiences in Palestine demonstrates that through the person of Jesus there really did work a power which exceeded his personal performance and must be seen as closely connected with the future evolution of humanity. It is this power which is given the name 'Messiah' in Hebrew and in Greek translation is named 'Christos'. But how can we understand the relationship between Jesus and the Christ Power without falling into the pattern of glorification?

A good answer to this question can be found in the message from the angel Michael about the several dimensions of life; this is the one which my colleague Ana Pogacnik received on September 16, 1996 and which has already been mentioned. The message confirms, that in addition to the three aspects which form the identity of every person, there are further dimensions; these influence a person's further evolution, playing a temporary role in their life and then disappearing again when they have fulfilled their task. Three such dimensions were explained:

• During childhood, there are different layers of time which exist parallel to each other. On the one hand, the child lives in the memories which it has brought with it out of the previous cycle of its development. On the other hand, the Spirit of the Time teaches it to understand the culture into which it is now born. From these are laid the foundations of the life which faces it. With the passage into puberty both layers bind themselves together and become the basis for the budding personality.

• Something similar happens in old age, i.e., before a person leaves incarnation. On the one hand, they go on living in the accustomed rhythm while externally the experiences which accompany the conclusion of life's course condense and are rounded off. At the same time, preparations are made for a new life on the spiritual plane where they will arrive when they have left the physical. In the course of this process the experiences and information which were gathered during the life now ending are impressed into the memory capacity of the soul so that they may be carried on through death into the future.

• A further dimension — one which interests us here — can enter a person's life if, during a particular phase of their development, a being approaches from the invisible realms of life, whose task it is to give that person some particular information or to teach them something special. Such a being may be a highly developed elemental who serves humans in the role of helpful companion. An angel or a spiritual master may fulfill a similar role, making contact with certain people and offering them spiritual direction. Such an additional dimension can open up when a person has become ready for it, and it can close again when it has fulfilled its purpose.

Jesus obviously experienced this sort of broadening of the dimensions in his thirtieth year. Before he was initiated into the relationship with 'his Father', he was an anonymous man from Nazareth. Then there came the revelation of this new relationship, which according to tradition happened during his baptism in Jordan. The gospels report that Jesus, after he had climbed up from the water, saw, "…the heavens torn apart and the Spirit, like a dove, descending on him. And a voice came from heaven, 'You are my Son, the Beloved; my favor rests on you.'" (Mark 1:10).

After his relationship with the 'Father' had been established — Jesus used the Aramaic expression 'Abba' which translates as 'Papa' — his way of life changed drastically. He began to go from town to town and teach the people publicly, "And his teaching made a deep impression on them because, unlike the scribes, he taught them with authority." (Mark 1:22). Soon afterwards he performed the first healing miracle. "The people were so astonished that they started asking one another what it all meant, saying, 'Here is a teaching that is new, and with authority behind it: he gives orders even to unclean spirits and they obey him.' And his reputation at once spread everywhere, through all the surrounding Galilean countryside." (Mark 1:27).

Jesus himself was conscious of the key significance of his relationship with the spiritual Being whom he called 'Father' and he spoke about it in public. In a conversation with a group of Jews, which is reported in the eighth chapter of the Gospel according to John, he is said to have characterized it in the following way: "... you will know that I am He and that I do nothing of my own accord. What I say is what the Father has taught me; he who sent me is with me, and has not left me to myself, for I always do what pleases him." (John 8:28). Two verses earlier he expresses it still more clearly: "... what I declare to the world I have learnt from him."

I would suggest that these words are not to be understood only as symbols, but as a description of the real relationship existing between Christ in the role of Master and Jesus as his pupil. In this saying the pupil confirms that Christ is constantly with him. He brings into the world only what is inspired by his Master. One can even understand Jesus to be saying that all the things which he reveals to the public in the form of words are messages which he has previously received through the inner voice of Christ.

In the relationship between a spiritual master and his pupil — as is the case in the connection between Christ and Jesus — a meeting takes place on a higher level which can only come about through constant self-testing and spiritual nurture on part of the pupil. The gospels report in several places how Jesus withdrew into the wilderness to pray and engage in conversations 'with his Father'. These were perceived by the apostles present to be fraught with deep emotion. Obviously Jesus was going through a process of inner dialogue with Christ, who was leading him into becoming One.

A section in the fourteenth chapter of the Gospel according to John tells us a great deal about this connection between Jesus and his spiritual Master. It deals with a three stage relationship, where the first stage can be described as 'Becoming One in the Heart'. It is described in the following way: "Philip said, 'Lord, show us the Father and then we shall be satisfied.' Jesus said to him, 'Have I been with you all this time, Philip, and you still do not know me? Anyone who has seen me has seen the Father, so how can you say, "Show us the Father"? Do you not believe that I am in the Father and the Father is in me?'" (John 14:8).

In the course of this process of 'Becoming One', in which a person can be involved during a period of their development, there comes a second step where there is an exchange between the pupil and the more highly evolved being. This enables the pupil to perform works which are beyond their own power, or to make speeches which they could not formulate on their own. This is accomplished by the power and wisdom of the spiritual master working through them. It is in this deeper sense that the speech with the disciples continues: "What I say to you I do not speak of my own accord; it is the Father, living in me, who is doing his works. You must believe me when I say that I am in the Father and the Father is in me; or at least believe it on the evidence of these works."

When the pupil has learned to connect with the master and do 'his' — i.e., the master's — works, they arrive at the third stage which is the mastery itself. Now they are capable of enabling others to perform their works. In harmony with this concept, this passage of John's Gospel continues: "In all truth I tell you, whoever believes in me will perform the same works as I do myself, and will perform even greater works, because I am going to the Father."

Faith in Jesus as the entry point to the learning process presented here is offered to all humanity. I might add that the last part of the above sentence may have been distorted. To correspond to the content of the speech, the saying must originally have carried the meaning: "... for I (myself) am becoming the Father."

As we have seen, the human being moves back and forth between different dimensions, whether or not we are conscious of it. I would describe the three dimensions as Earthhuman, Soulhuman and Godhuman. In particular critical phases, these can be broadened to include further dimensions: for example, through readiness on the part of highly evolved elemental beings or the spiritual world to give a person support. This may happen so that they can take decisive steps on their personal path of development, or so that they can perform some work which is meaningful for the evolution of the whole of humanity.

Jesus could become Christ during the last three years of his work on earth because he went through all the necessary changes to unite the above-named three dimensions of the human being within himself. In consequence, he has not only introduced a new phase into the process of human evolution and imparted the impulse for the future development of humanity; after he had left the earthly plane, he also remains present as Christ for all eternity.

Chapter 11

The Christ Archetype
Across Cultures

In the previous chapter I tried to demolish the pattern of exclusivity which places Jesus as the Messiah, i.e., World Savior above humanity. Among other ills perpetrated by insistence on the messianic idea is the fact that the message, which should be brought home to the *whole* of humankind through the teaching and works of Jesus, is made unacceptable to many non-Christian cultures, both in the past and now. The same is true for many individual persons in our culture who, quite rightly, do not wish to renounce the freedom to shape their own way from out of their own center, without having to bow to an outside authority.

I think my experiences attest that the Being which in the gospel texts is called 'Christ' is concerned with the evolution of humankind as a whole. As I have emphasized several times, I see his role as that of leading humankind into that phase of their evolution which is characterized by the independence of the individual. This process was set in motion many thousands of years ago and is still not concluded. It follows that this impulse which guides and accompanies humanity through the events of our evolution cannot be limited to the time-span of Jesus' incarnation in Palestine.

To honor the Western tradition into which I was born, I should like to continue to use the term 'Christ' in reference to the divine impulse which inspires the future evolution of humankind. However, to avoid personalizing too strongly, I have decided on the expression 'Christ Power'. The way I feel about it, this title provides a good balance between the two aspects of his presence. On the one hand, this is an inspirational power which penetrates and surrounds humankind to promote our further development, and on the other hand it is also a Being from the universal dimensions which performs its inspirational role consciously and out of personal love.

In the well-known prologue to John's Gospel, the mighty Being I have described as Christ Power is characterized in the following way: "The Word was the real light that gives light to everyone; he was coming into the world. He was in the world that had come into being through him, and the world did not recognize him."

In the gospel tradition, Christ was that very same Power or Being which accompanied Jesus through the three years of his public works in Palestine. Jesus associated with it during this time and lovingly addressed it as his Father. Jesus was however conscious that these matters concerned a time dimension which would greatly exceed his own lifespan. On one occasion, when his countrymen pressed him with questions about his person, he spoke to them in the following way: "In all truth I tell you, before Abraham was, I am." (John 8:58). One should note that for the Jews, Abraham symbolized the utmost limit of the years through they which could trace their race.

The earliest indication of Christ Power in the history of human evolution can be found in the biblical context of the myth of Adam and Eve. This concerns the so-called 'Fall into Sin' through which humankind lost its place in paradise. I may immediately add however that I can see no trace of sin in it, but rather a milestone on the evolutionary path of humankind[1]. As long as humankind remained in paradise we were embedded in the earthly and cosmic Wholeness through our apprehension of an unlimited and self-evident truth. To speak in the language of the Bible, after humans had tasted the apple from the tree of the knowledge of good and evil, they had to leave behind their paradisiacal consciousness. From then on people had to learn to think independently, and decide for themselves between what is ethically and morally justifiable in the sense of being life-promoting, and what is destructive of life. From a place of personal love in their own center, they must learn to build whole new relationships to earth, to the divine, and their own fellow men and women. One can rightly speak of the ultimate all-encompassing learning program!

To create the most favorable circumstances for the actualization of this wonderful task, humankind was led through the so-called 'Expulsion from Eden' into a habitat which was quite differently fashioned and much tougher and more concretely molded. This was in no way to punish humans but rather it was the divine response to our first step towards independence of the self. The God of Genesis himself commented with words of delight on the great change which was accomplished under the tree of knowledge: "... the man has become like one of us in knowing good from evil." (Gen. 3:22).

This new habitat 'outside paradise' in which we find ourselves today is supportive of our new line of evolution because its tough, material consistency lets us feel the consequences of our actions directly in our own body or life circumstances. More and more this puts us in the position of being able to judge what is life promoting — i.e., what is favorable to our development and the development of our environment and inspires joy — and what presents us

---

1 See the chapter, 'Der ethisch-moralische Aspekt der Menschwerdung' in my book *Schule der Geomantie*.

with the reverse of these qualities. In consequence we are the sole authority for our life's decisions and no longer subject to externally imposed ethical, moral and religious norms and commandments. Step by step, we can think and act out of our own freedom and creativity.

The earliest evidence of Christ Power which I have discovered is from the megalithic culture in Portugal. This is in a complex stone circle from the third millennium before our era. It is situated in the neighborhood of Evora. Its official name is the 'Cromlech dos Almendres'. It is not a regularly formed stone circle, but consists of about forty standing stones arranged in a circular manner, some in groups close together and some standing independently in their own space.

The stone circle of Dos Almendres is erected on a power point which works on a variety of planes. One of them acts as a strong exhalation center through which earthly forces stream out and distribute themselves over the earth's surface. One could picture it as something like a volcano. The related inhalation center is situated roughly 80 kilometers eastward and is known as the stone circle of Do Xares. There, cosmic forces flow into the interior of the earth.

The second function of the stone circle at Dos Almendres is to act as a storehouse of forces and information. I can use it to look into the interior of the hill to perceive the nature of its composition. Further, this storehouse makes possible an intensive exchange of forces between earth and its galactic environment. All these exceptional geomantic features were used by the circle's builders to create a unique place of ritual which served to initiate people into the secrets of the several dimensions of life.

In October 1996, I was leading a seminar on the country around the Center for Human Ecology 'Tamera' in western Portugal, and I visited the stone circle together with my daughter Ana. After we had experienced the several dimensions of the place and its astounding riches, I asked Ana to question the angel whom we describe as the 'Angel of Memories' about its original function. For several years Ana has communicated with this cosmic consciousness which guards the memories of various earthly cultures.

In summary, the answer told us that the culture of that time pursued two goals with the erection of this complex stone circle. One was that each single stone should be so oriented that it resonated with the power source in its position. The whole composition worked to support the operation of the exhalation center so that its action was enhanced and enriched.

The second function of the stone placements was to represent a 'tree of life', in which certain groups of stones and individual stones respectively represented various aspects of life. However, the stones bear no visible signs of their role in the framework of this 'tree of life'; the corresponding symbols, information and color qualities were impressed on them in a purely spiritual-energetic way. The people of the former culture made pilgrimages from all over the country to this 'circle of life' to experience, in the mirror of the stones, the different dimensions of the life in which they participated. They also gained a deeper insight into the changes in their lives.

The stones of the circle of life make three groups. The first is bound up with the process of birth and the building of personal identity. The second is devoted to the events of life and growth. Within this second group there are also stones representing other dimensions of the fabric of life: for example, those of the angels, of the elemental beings, of other earth evolutions and so on. The role of the third group of standing stones is to represent the transition to a new plane of existence, i.e., the process of dying, by which a person swings back onto the plane of the soul. In addition to the three groups I have mentioned, there are further stones devoted to the forces of the four elements —

water, earth, air and fire — which form the basic structure of life's fabric.

Because I was already working on preparations for the present book when I visited the stone circle of Dos Almendres, I was especially interested to see whether there were stones devoted to the Christ Power within the 'tree of life'. In my experience certainly, it plays an important role within the framework of the fabric of life. I found the corresponding stone through meditation. It is supported in its function by two stones at its side. When I looked inside to see what information was impressed within, I was moved in a most astounding way in my own inner space. The space feels dark with a sense of reddish brown. After some time a white point emerges in its center. This slowly begins to shine and finally takes on the form of an embryo. The association which came to mind was that of the black Madonna with the shining Christ Child in her womb.

The other two stones make a three cornered composition with the first and display quite contrasting information. One shows a gray eye in the face of an ancient, dying man; the other, in contrast, displays a fruit which shines with the most lively colors. The intuition which surfaced alongside the vision caused me to remember the transformation process which Jesus underwent as exemplar and which leads from death to resurrection and onto a new evolutionary plane. I have described in chapter 6 how decisive this three stage transformation process is for the future evolution of the human being. It concerns a determining aspect for the unfolding of humankind, one for which Christ Power stands as the source of inspiration and leadership.

In the Indian culture of old Mexico I found a second example of the global, culturally unbounded significance of the consciousness which I have described as Christ Power. On the occasion of an Idriart festival[2] (situated in Cuernavaca in the federal state of Morelos), I was invited to

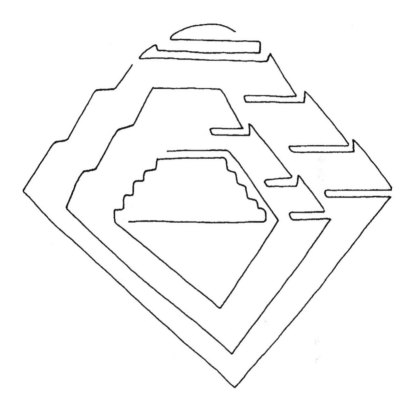

*A step pyramid from Tihuacan, Mexico
with its light pole pointing into the depths of the earth.*

do earth healing work on the surrounding landscape and present my findings to the festival group. The first pyramid complex which I was to investigate was situated to the south of Cuernavaca near Xochicalco. The pyramids stand on the ridge of a mountain at the foot of which there extends a round volcanic lake which represents the feminine center — the yin pole — of the surrounding landscape. The complex of pyramids, which consists of two larger and several smaller pyramids, represents the ritual superstructure of this feminine power point.

I went deep within myself in front of the pyramids and to my surprise I became aware of another pyramid which had a light body and whose positioning was the exact opposite of a physical pyramid. Its base was turned to heaven and its point directed to the center of the earth. I should emphasize that a polarized physical-etheric structure of this kind was also to be found in other Mexican pyramids which I later visited. The Angel of Earth Healing whom Ana questioned also confirmed that this configuration was fundamental to the pyramid construction of that culture.

The physical pyramid built from stone represents the earthly forces which are borne up into the cosmos through the pyramid's step-form construction. In contrast, the reversed light pyramid incorporates the cosmic forces which dive deep into the body of earth. In this way every pyramid brings about an active exchange between the earthly and cosmic forces, in the middle of which humankind used to stand with its rituals and festivals,.

This configuration creates an archetypal pattern which is almost identical to the cosmogram which Jesus used to represent the new plane of human evolutionary consciousness which he initiated by his activity in Palestine. In

---

2 The 'Idriart' Foundation was founded by my brother Miha Pogačnik in order to establish bridges between different lands and cultures through the medium of art.

*The upward directed gaze of the wolf and the downward flight of
the eagle symbolize the two directions in which Mexican pyramid
construction is oriented —
the silhouettes of the pyramids are to be seen beside the two beasts.
Seated in a balancing role
between the two directions is the human being.
(From a clay seal of the Toltec culture.)*

Chapter 3, I described how I discovered it through the story of the miraculous feeding of the multitudes, and I sketched it in connection with the invisible archetypal pattern of the gospels (see illustration on p.59). It is a lemniscate, in the middle of which stands humankind. With one of its two spiral arcs it makes the connection with the cosmic pole, with the other with the earthly pole of the world wholeness. This illustrates the new covenant which Jesus sought to anchor within human consciousness. As the sign of perfect balance, he allows us to connect ourselves anew, both with the cosmic and the earthly extensions of our universe — and without losing our Self in the process.

The two shrines which stand beside each other on the great pyramid of Xochicalco are still well preserved. The one on the right hand is adorned with eight feathered snakes and dedicated to the cosmic forces. In its center I see a powerful etheric flame focused. The left-hand one is dedicated to the earthly pole. Within it I can see a vertical pathway leading into the depths of the earth; this represents the connection with the world of the ancestors who dwell in a specific dimension of the earth's core.

An inner chamber discovered during excavations represents the third sacred space of the complex. Within it stood three sculptured, decorated stelae which today one can admire in the Anthropological Museum in Mexico City. The stela of Quetzacoatl displays a pleasant, almost white and Caucasian type of face. He is the God Hero who was temporarily defeated and disappeared to the east; but in the future is expected to return from the west. When I projected my consciousness into the stela, I experienced an admonishment in the center of my being, similar to the one I had with the 'Archetypal Christ Stone' in the megalithic stone circle in Portugal. Since the pyramids of Xochicalco are relatively late, having been first erected between the years 1,000 and 1,500 AD, several millennia stretch between the two complexes. How tragic that the Christians who conquered the country and destroyed the high Indian civilization could not recognize the seal of the Christ presence in these cultures!

I had another experience in Tibet where my findings were amazingly similar to those in the Central American pyramids. The first occurred in August 1997 when I was actively engaged in another Idriart festival in Katmandu and Lhasa. While listening to my brother Miha Pogacnik playing the violin in a Tibetan monastery in Nepal — the most beautiful of the Bach solo sonatas was resonating around us — I noticed that, invisibly, an archetypal pattern had arisen in the room which resembled the above mentioned cosmogram of Jesus. The pattern first formed a spiral connection with earth, and then with heaven.

The monastery where this happened was one of the many founded by Tibetan Buddhists in exile. Their spiritual-energetic atmosphere is essentially distinct from the Hindu temples which stand in their direct neighborhood. In the native shrines, manifestations of an extravagant mixture of different colors and light offer themselves to the inner eye. In contrast, the places whose spiritual care is the Buddhists' responsibility display a pure emptiness where cosmogramic forms take shape in the ether during rituals. Among them I have sometimes perceived the above-mentioned 'cosmogram of the feeding of the four and five thousand'. In the Buddhist tradition one finds a corresponding form in the well-known Dorje — the indestructible diamond which stands as the object symbolizing the unchangeable, clear essence of reality which lies at the foundation of everything. If it is held upright —for thus my inner sight beholds the symbol — it resembles two crowns, one of which points downwards, the other upwards. At their center they are bound fast together to make a wholeness.

I made a further observation of the same sort in the celebrated monastery of Drepung, in the neighborhood of Lhasa. As a prelude, the festival group was playing

European classical music for the monks in one of the court-
yards of the monastery; among them there were works of
Bach and Mozart, and Renaissance songs were also performed. Afterwards a large group of young novices recited
sutras. After a little while a dark shining shell-like form
began to take shape in the earthly realm underneath the
courtyard; this represents the relationship with the earthly
forces; finally a similar form, but of bright silver, took shape
in the atmosphere above the group; this stands for the cosmic pole. In the next phase, in the middle space between
the two etheric forms, and thus centered on the group of
young monks, a focused crystal space began to build; this
stands for the role of humankind which is to bind the two
poles together.

When my brother Miha Pogacnik teaches the 'active
hearing' of music, he always emphasizes that the secret of
the individualization of the human being is most clearly
inscribed within the fabric of classical western music.
Individualization is a process which is guided by the Christ
Power, among others. I suspect that it is contact with classical European music which arouses that precise aspect of
Buddhism which corresponds to the western concept of
Christ Power. It revealed itself to me — as happened when
the novices were reciting in Drepung — as the cosmogram
of the new covenant with humanity which Jesus demonstrated through the feeding of the two multitudes.

In one of the Tibetan monasteries, among several six-
foot high gilded statues of Buddha, we were shown the
'Buddha of the Future'. He is called Maitreya Buddha. In
the theosophical tradition he is equated with the Cosmic
Christ whom Jesus was accustomed to address as "My
Father."

In all fairness, I must add that the same cosmogram of
the new covenant, which stands for the reconnection of
humanity in balance with heaven and earth, may also be
perceived during the Christian mass. In the first chapter I

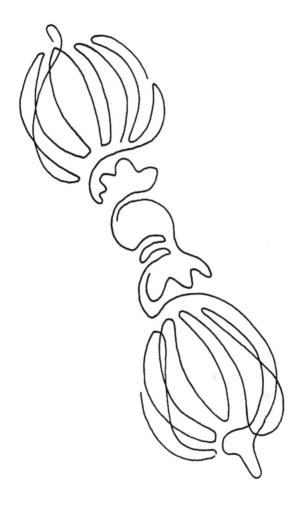

The Dorje, a Buddhist symbolic object,
which resembles the archetypal pattern
which I observed in the Tibetan temple.

have pointed out that in my experience it did not matter
which church celebrated the ritual of the Eucharist or who
was the officiating priest, but that on each occasion there
was an outpouring of a positive love-filled power which I
first perceived in the form of a Christ figure. This descends
during the communion and gives of its powers to all present. In my later observations it was shown that the Christ
figure, whose emergence at first so astonished me, is only a
sign to identify the outpouring power. What is most decisive is the emotional quality which comes to expression
there, and in which all present participate.

After our connection with the spiritual-*cosmic* aspect of
Wholeness has found its expression through the celebration
of the Eucharist, one would expect that the further course
of the mass would see a reconnection with the *earthly*
aspect. Unfortunately, this does not happen. The obstructive patterns about which I wrote in the eighth chapter are
working here in the most destructive way. I perceive this
effect to be such that soon after the joyful outpouring of the
Christ Power, a force emerges from the earth which wraps
the assembled congregation in an unhealthy feeling of sorrow. This can feel dark and threatening.

At first I was so inspired by the blessing left behind during the mass that I quite overlooked the reverse side.
However, after I had discovered the pattern of division into
good and evil in the gospel texts and the general obstruc-
tiveness in respect of earth's systems, the experience of this
negativity arising from the earth would not let me alone.
For quite some time I was tormented by it, and then I went
after its secret.

In my first observations of this dark power, I perceived
the figure of the adversary which is described in the Biblical
texts as 'Satan' or 'the Devil'. Just as the blessing of Christ
descends in a vertical axis and is directed towards the
priest's place in front of the altar, so the dark contrary
power has a specific focal point from which it arises from

the earth in a reverse direction. Usually its place is found in a remote corner of the church, one to which nobody pays attention.

My later observations have established that the supposed adversarial figure must really be a distorted aspect of Christ Power and in no way an opponent who threatens the latter's light-filled rule over earth. When I had worked through all the dark layers with which the 'Adversary' covers itself, and through all those dark layers that it carries when it rises out of the earth, I arrived once again at the figure of Christ. As counterpart to that figure which descends with its blessing from above, it climbs up from the earth hunched under the load of sin and darkness which were and are projected onto the earthly pole of the world wholeness by our pattern of division into black and white.

This is obviously the same Christ cosmogram which I had experienced in the Tibetan temple. However it must have been mutilated by the Christian culture of the last two thousand years. Of the two basic elements which form the cosmogram, the earthly element is obstructed and its function distorted. Instead of facilitating the reconnection with the life systems of earth, the spirit of earth has become a scapegoat on which are laden all those forces which human beings reject.

The Christian Church has not rendered us capable of dealing with these forces by using our own creativity (even with divine help). They are none other than the forces of earth and nature which work through our body, our Self and our consciousness. Within the framework of a Christian upbringing we have not been taught to love and understand them as an expression of the wisdom of Earth.

Fortunately, during one of my visits to Brazil in November 1997 I experienced a Christian ritual which did not invoke the conflict described above. This was a ritual which arose in the primeval forests of the Amazon at the beginning of our present century. The mass consists of var-

ious hymns which are sung and danced by all the participants — children, women and men — and are accompanied by cheerful, rhythmic music. The people dance in a
constantly repeating pattern, two steps to the right side,
two steps to the left and again two steps to the right.

I also experienced the 'Amazonian Mass' in a larger community in the southern part of the state of Minas Gerais.
This community bears the name of the 'Matutu Institution'
and is deeply engaged in the protection of forests and
waters. For this purpose they have erected a circular chamber whose roof is carried by a single central wooden pillar.

Just before I was invited to the ritual, I visited the chamber and realized that its vital energies are clearly polarized:
the forces of the right-hand half have a masculine character
and lead heavenwards. The left-hand half has a feminine
polarization and leads towards the innermost of the earth.
In contrast the center feels balanced and vibrates in a yin-
yang rhythm. I came to understand the energetic composition of the room when the members of the community
gathered for the ritual. The men always sang and danced on
the right, the women on the left-hand side. The children
had their place in the area where the energy was equalized
between the men and women, girls to the rear, boys to the
front of the chamber. The musicians sat around the pillar in
the center. I went to sit with them so that, from an inner
perspective, I could observe the progress of the ritual clearly. To ensure a Christian framework, the ritual begins and
ends with an 'Our Father' in which all join. In between, for
about an hour without a break, individual hymns are sung
and danced.

I had a unique experience. In contrast to the usual mass
where I must persistently battle with unclarities, from the
first hymn to the last my inner sight was never clouded.
Only in one song was a veil laid over the inner picture.
With a little effort I found out that the hymn was dedicated to a nymph, a being of the water element. Obviously

there had been an attempt to hide its true content because of a fear of being reproached for heathenism.

Accompanying the first hymns an inner picture formed. It begins with a group of tall palms, one of which bears a ripe coconut. The nut falls to earth and opens into four parts. From its white kernel white ribbons stream out across the earth to the four points of the compass, making an isosceles cross which embraces the whole world. From the center of this world-cross there again grow three palms, one of which bears a ripe coconut. The nut falls to earth.... A coconut carries within it as archetype the characteristic features of the Christ cosmogram which accompanies the feeding of the two multitudes: the rough brown exterior of the nut stands for the earthly extensions of the Being, the sweet white interior for the spiritual-soul extensions. Both are united in the body of a fruit.

During one of the hymns a wonderful feminine figure took the place of the three palms in the middle of the white cross. I saw her as Mary-Sophia, the feminine aspect of Christ. There was also a group of songs which drew my attention to the center of my heart. From there was offered to my vision an indescribably joyful outpouring of all possible colors, spreading over everything around.

When the community came to the last hymn, I felt Christ's presence in me and around me; it took no form but made itself known by its unique spiritual-emotional quality. Not only we, the participants, but our whole world around us were suffused with happiness and spirit.

Chartres Cathedral in its spatial form.

Chapter 12

Sacred Geomancy[1]: Expression of Christ Power on Earth

To correct the impression that everything in the Christian culture relating to Christ Power has gone awry over the last two thousand years, I should like to introduce two outstanding examples which demonstrate to the contrary. For the first, our journey takes us to France and to the Cathedral of Chartres. Without any doubt, this is one of the most important cathedral constructions of the Middle Ages, one which introduced a wholly new architectural style into the history of European art: the style of the Gothic Cathedral. Chartres Cathedral is not only a cultural creation of the first rank, but it was one of the most visited places of pilgrimage during the Middle Ages.

Viewed geomantically, the cathedral stands on a power point similar to the stone circle of Dos Almendres in Portugal, namely on a 'volcano' from which the life-power streams from the interior of the earth. It also acts as one of earth's exhalation centers, with a very powerful output. The whole countryside is nourished by the pure and subtle life-powers which distribute themselves over the surrounding area from this spot. The cathedral stands in the middle of

---

1 The concept of 'Geomancy' is derived from ge (Greek) — the earth — and manteia (Greek) — prophecy. From the 18th-century onwards it has been employed to describe a type of divination, and since the end of the 19th-century used in the sense of interaction with the forces of the earth.

this exhalation-stream, although its structure partially hinders its free effusion into space.

The construction has two stories. In the area below ground level lies a crypt which resembles a broad tunnel running under the whole building. Its entrance is under the north tower, its exit under the corresponding southern one. These two towers are the only ones completed of the nine which were begun. They both stand on the side of the main facade.

The physical cathedral stands above the vault of the crypt. Terraced in a series of ogive arches striving aloft, it represents the powers of earth growing towards the spiritual dimension of the Whole. Through the architectural magic of Gothic forms which conjure the impression of weight-less space, the world of earth is lifted towards the world of light.

When I view the physical construction with my inner sight, I see that it is complemented by a cathedral of light which points symmetrically below into the depths of the earth. It looks as if a heavenly cathedral has been built from above downwards in the direction of the earth's center, as earthly complement. This is an interpenetration of the earthly and spiritual-cosmic forces similar to the ones I rediscovered in the Indian pyramids of Central America.

The stone walls of a Gothic cathedral are built so that they incline gently to the outside in order to imprint the building with the feeling of an upward striving toward heaven. Despite this, the construction does not fall apart, because a series of buttresses support the walls from the outside. According to my intuition, the enormous forces which are caught and led into the earth by these buttresses serve as the etheric construction material for the downward pointing cathedral of light. These forces can be experienced in the crypt which has been mentioned above. With the cathedral as with the kingdom of heaven, a person must connect themselves with earth in order to experience the

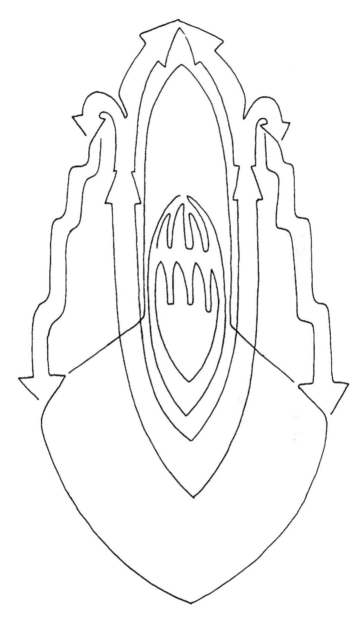

The upwardly rising forces of the physical cathedral
are led below by the flying buttresses and form
a cathedral of light, reversed as in a mirror.
(Chartres, France, 12th century)

powers of heaven, just as Jesus said.

I should add that Chartres' holy image, a black Madonna[2], was kept in the crypt. People also brought the sick to spend a few days and nights in the crypt so that they might be healed. For those making the pilgrimage to Chartres, the progress through the crypt was, in the truest sense of the word, fundamental.

The pilgrims entered the crypt from the ground floor of the northern tower. They walked praying and singing through the whole U-shaped tunnel and climbed up again into the light through the stairwell in the southern clock tower. This was a re-experience of the nine months that they had dwelt in the body of their mother, and a renewed passage through the process of birth. Just as the soul is led by an angelic hand through the different planes of incarnation, so the pilgrim, led by the beam of angelic light, climbed down into the darkness of the crypt's womb[3].

After they had re-experienced all the pre-natal phases by making their passage through the crypt, the pilgrims climbed out through the tower of birth into the daylight and the sphere of material life. The 'newborns' found themselves beneath the southern tower where one can perceive the presence of the nature spirits and elemental beings which represent the forces of earth and make possible the incarnation of humankind. They are shown in sculpted forms on the outer wall of the tower.

The passage through the crypt at Chartres reminds us of Jesus' requirement that we should become as little children in order to arrive at self-knowledge. As explained in the seventh chapter, we gain access to the voice of our own soul when we transcend our culturally and socially conditioned imprint, and in spirit seek the way back to our own source which wells freely on the other side of birth. The passage

---

2 Unfortunately, it was burnt during the French Revolution.
3 Today, the original entrance is built over to accommodate the site of a souvenir shop.

through the crypt is accomplished within the space of the etheric light cathedral, and therefore in the space which holds the cosmic quality, and so it is truly suited to represent the space where the soul originates.

In the neighborhood of the old altar the figure of the Madonna of Chartres is portrayed in a brightly colored stained-glass window. She wears a robe of heavenly blue, the Christ Child in contrast one of an earthy brown, so that together they represent the holy marriage of heaven and earth. After I had found a nearby acupuncture point through which I could best enter into connection with the Madonna, she unexpectedly spoke to me in words which were steeped in a feeling of the deepest mystery. Quickly I wrote them down in my notebook: "The mystery of the Second Coming of Christ among humankind lies in this, that it is uninterruptedly in progress. The cathedral is so constructed that it enables the Second Coming of Christ to occur at every moment — not as a future event, but now and always, when the principle of the eternal Soul joins with the principle of the eternal Earth."

My second example comes from Venice. Here I am thinking of the Basilica of St. Mark — called San Marco — in whose rear courtyard the story of this book began. Like the Cathedral of Chartres, the Basilica of San Marco is centered around a vital-energetic exhalation point. This is part of the place's respiration system, which is composed of an inhalation and exhalation center. The center which serves as inhalation point for the cosmic forces is near the Church of San Alvise, situated on the northeastern edge of Venice. The forces which are inhaled there undergo a process of change and harmonization with earth's frequencies in its interior, and are sent out through the exhalation center and distributed as life-inspiring forces over the earth's surface. For more than a thousand years the exhalation center has been situated in the middle of the Basilica of San Marco, spanned by a construction formed of five gold-covered cupolas.

One would expect that construction over such a sensitive site would represent a bitter disturbance of the life-sustaining function of earth's systems. In this case the disturbance was neutralized, because the basilica was built and correctly harmonized as an instrument through which the outward streaming forces could be caught, potentized and led out again into the environment. They are not only strengthened by the process, but enriched with additional soul-spiritual information. Consequently, the presumed infringement on earth's systems would have been more than offset if the geomantic structure of the basilica had not been mutilated during the last two centuries, causing its true function to be quite extensively paralyzed[4].

However, our present consideration of the Basilica of San Marco is not directly concerned with its vital-energetic effects and problems. Our concern is rather to find out how the culture in the Middle Ages made it possible for people to experience the presence of Christ inwardly, so that they could progress further along their path towards individualization.

To better understand the role of the basilica as it relates to the Christ experience, we should direct our attention to the presbytery where there is another power center which makes an essential contribution to the basilica's whole effect. This one is a 'heart center' which is situated deep in the earth under the altar space. It is put together from two sub-centers, of which the main center serves to expand the forces and the second center to draw them together, so that they act like a heart muscle in their common rhythm of alternating contraction and expansion.

Expressed poetically, the role of the heart center in earth's systems is to bathe the life on earth's surface in the loving power of Mother Earth. Just as all things are held in

---

4 More precise information is contained in my book, *Geheimnis Venedig: Modell einer vollkommenen Stadt*.

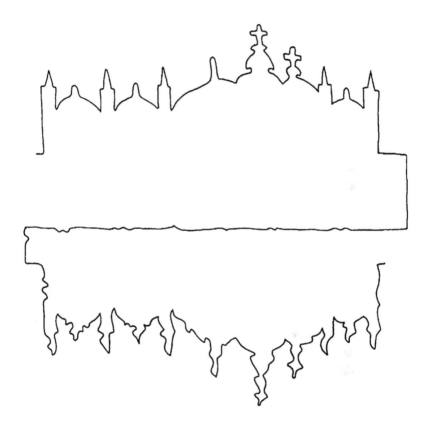

The facade of the Basilica of San Marco in Venice
mirrored in the waters of the flooded marketplace.

their place by the force of gravity, so all beings who inhabit Earth are granted the sense of her Being through the power of her love. One can compare the working of the heart center to the circulation of the blood. Just as the blood exits from the heart and returns there after flowing through the body, so the etheric stream flows out from the heart center and conveys to features in the landscape necessary information regarding their identity within Earth's systems.

The heart power which has its source in the area of the presbytery, and the life power which streams out from the exhalation center situated in the middle of the body of the basilica, together represent the two sources from which power and information is fed to the basilic space. The space itself forms the counterpole, a storehouse through which the up-welling forces are caught and transformed. The basilic space is so shaped that it offers the perfect instrument for the forces streaming there to play their 'music'.

The floor plan of the basilic space forms a cross with arms of equal length — the archetypal symbol for the equilibrium of spirit and matter. Above the four arms of the cross and above their intersection in the middle rise the curves of the five magnificent cupolas, adorned with bright mosaics laid on gilded surfaces. Everything which presents corners and angles on the floor of the basilica below is translated in the ceiling above into the rounded forms of arches, vaults or cupolas. So there comes about a change in the nature of the space, and this would remain on a purely formal level if the powers of heart and life were not drawn into the process, as I have described above.

The influence of the forces of the place — and in this the forces stemming from the polarized heart center are decisive — causes still further dimensions to arise within the physical space. These are invisible to the outward eye, but for the inward feelings they are not less present than the physical features. Whoever really involves themselves in the

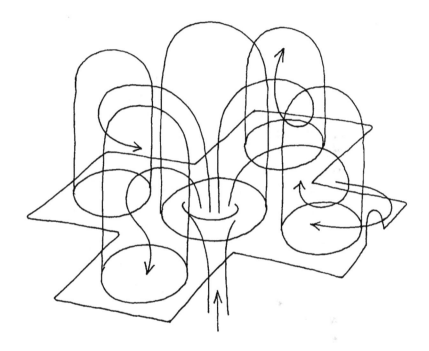

The five cupolas of San Marco and the exhalation center in the middle of the basilic space.
The cupolas stimulate the exhaled forces to circulate through the space of the Basilica.

quality of the space can hardly avoid the feeling that they are being carried by its several dimensional nature into space of a different quality. It is that quality of space and life which Jesus has described in the concept of the 'kingdom of heaven', or 'kingdom of God'.

The several dimensions of space within the basilica are created because the transformative tension between the angular forms of the floor plan and the roundness of the cupolas is potentized with information and forces from vital-energetic sources and is extended on the space's subtle planes. This enables the basilic space to help people who are sunk deep in inner silence, in prayer or some other heart-felt attitude, to transcend their one-sided concentration on the material plane and experience their own several dimensions. It is through this several layered nature of Being that people are offered the space to become free, and freely unfold in the direction of the future vision of humanity. Where this freedom is lacking, we are dependent on the exploitation and extravagant waste of the forces of life and feeling as the only means of living life fully.

When, immersed in the several dimensions of San Marco's space — which models the realization of the kingdom of heaven on earth — I observed the effect of the quality of this space on myself, I established that my head was resonating with the square shaped floor plan of the basilica, my heart however with the curvatures of the cupolas. Everything is reversed: what in the basilic space is below, for people is above, and what is below for people, is above in San Marco. Thus, on the one hand there is a correspondence between the basilica and the people who are standing inside it, and on the other hand there is a creative tension which comes about through their experience of the reversal of the poles. The basilica has something specific to teach people.

When I wanted to pursue this question, I had the sudden feeling that my head was inclining very far forwards

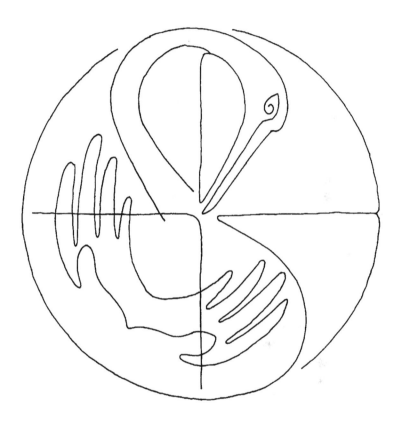

The pelican bestowing its heart forces
— a Christ symbol — from the altar of
St. Margaret's Church in Kranj, Slovenia.
(Drawn by the author, Kalkstein, 1990)

— more than my neck would ever allow — and was bending down to my heart center. Only a swan with its long neck could manage something like that! The process went still further. My head dived into the middle of my heart and there disappeared! Whatever would visitors to the basilica think when they suddenly saw me standing there headless?

As I waited there with my head in my heart, there came about that change in me which corresponds to the change in the basilica from its physical space to its several dimensional form. It felt as if I was immersed with my head under crystal clear water — though I had no difficulty breathing. The 'angular nature' of my mental pattern became rounded. Suddenly my head felt so light that it began to rise up like an air bubble along my spinal column until it finally found itself once again in the place assigned to it by nature. I was no longer headless.

The message of this incident is supported by my experience and can best be understood if one remembers that the teaching of Christ through Jesus sought to reach humankind in the exact same epoch when Roman culture was bringing the ancient discovery of logical thought to penetrate all realms of public and private life. On the one hand, it is important that one's sense of inner independence should be supported by one's capacity for logical thinking. On the other hand, should logic degenerate to an insipid rationality, there is the danger that it will clip the wings of the soul.

The teaching of the kingdom of heaven on earth, announced by Jesus, demonstrates how the danger of a superficial rationality can be prevented through the infusion of love. However, what is meant here by love is not a mere feeling or a care for those nearest to us, as demanded by social norms. It concerns far more the heart forces through which the voice of the soul can reveal itself by using the intuition, which is once again in direct connection with the human being's divine Self. If, before uttering their thoughts and releasing them in action, one lets them run through the heart so that they are enriched by the intuition and experienced as they broaden out into the several dimensions of being, then the danger which accompanies logical thinking is overcome.

A space like the Basilica of San Marco which was the goal of millions of pilgrims enabled many generations to be warned of this danger and experience in their subconscious "the Father's" guidance on how to overcome it — insofar as they were incapable of understanding it consciously. This prepared humankind for the New Age in which we are entirely delivered from the dangers of reason and its sister, egocentric thinking.

Chapter 13

Cinderella: a Folk Tale of Human Evolution

Translator's note. The Germanic story of Cinderella, given here, differs from the French/Italian version familiar to English readers. The differences are significant. In the English version, Cinderella is a hapless victim of circumstance who must be rescued by a fairy godmother, i.e., a power outside of herself; in the German version, she is a young woman who, facing the same circumstances, has the initiative to plant a hazel twig on her mother's grave and thereby prepares herself for her eventual elevation to a new plane of being. The twig grows into a miraculous tree which takes the place of the fairy godmother in providing the means for Cinderella to attend the prince's ball. It is worth remarking that in European folk lore, the hazel is a magic tree and sacred to the Earth Goddess. In Irish legend the Salmon of Wisdom gained its powers because it swallowed the hazel nuts which fell into the pool where it lay.

While I was writing the previous chapter, I became aware that Christ's presence must have needed other ways to reveal itself to people during the centuries of ecclesiastical rule. The four canonical gospels, which passed for its official expression, were too confused to transmit the several dimensions of Christ's message in all their fullness. This unhappy circumstance is to be ascribed on the one hand to those patterns of obstruction in the gospel texts which have already been described, and on the other to the rigidity of ecclesiastical dogmas which prevented any free communication about Christ's message.

During my inward preparations for the decoding of the hidden 'Fifth Gospel', I had already had a dream which I sensed as a demand that I not limit myself to the study of the gospel texts. I should also lend an ear to the wisdom of Sophia. Through the centuries She has supported people in their efforts to maintain their connection with the Christ Power. Her voice did not usually speak through writings and church dogma but through the oral folk traditions which, among other forms, found expression in folk tales and fairy stories.

In the above-mentioned dream I was the son of a forester. All day long I dragged heavy bundles of dead wood to our hut on the edge of the forest. A stream flowed not far from the hut. One day, when I came to its bank with a heavy load of wood under my right arm, I noticed that a pair of iron pliers was jammed between the sticks of wood. I put out my left hand to draw it out of the bundle as I began to cross, and then I noticed an iron ring on my ring finger.

At that very moment the ring slipped from my finger and fell into the waters of the stream. I did not want to let go of my load so near to the end of my journey and I decided that I would go back and look for the ring later. However, when I had reached my goal and deposited the bundle of wood in my father's courtyard, I sat myself down upon it, overcome with pain and sorrow. I asked myself why I must perform such drudgery without ever seeing any clear meaning in my task. And so I forgot about the ring. In the meantime it had become dusk. Suddenly remembering, I sprang to my feet to seek for the lost ring. But the channel of the stream had become too dark, and so I had to give up all hope of finding the ring again.

When I awoke, still overcome with a feeling of the importance of finding the ring again, some elements of the dream were immediately clear: the *iron* ring and the *iron* pliers symbolized the ruling spirit of our age. Because materialism played the decisive role in its formation, it is called the Iron Age — in distinction to the previous Bronze and Stone Ages respectively.

The ring and the pliers symbolize two complementary tools of our consciousness. The pliers, with their ability to seize an individual element and draw it out of the Wholeness — like a nail from a piece of wood — is an excellent symbol for rational, analytical thinking. In contrast, the ring, with its rounded, inclusive form, stands for the quality of intuition and the sensitive experience of the mysteries of life.

The loss of the ring principle and a simultaneous, progressive limitation to the pliers principle are characteristic of the Iron Age. In consequence our human feeling for the all-inclusive wholeness of life and our own being has fallen by the wayside. The result is to splinter the Wholeness into countless pieces, every single one of which we can certainly 'seize on' with the pliers of our rational thought, but these pliers cannot make the happy connection with 'the ring of wholeness'.

To return to the voice of Sophia, my attention was drawn to Snow White, the Sleeping Beauty, Red Riding Hood and Cinderella. They are the most important heroines in the fairy tales out of the Middle Ages which were written down from folk traditions in the 19th century by the Brothers Grimm. In their picture language lie buried those original patterns of humankind's evolution through which the feminine aspect of Christ becomes Word. In this sense, I feel their message to be the twin of the message in the gospel texts, complementary and also further extending them.

The story of Cinderella tells how the human being is splintered into individual parts which forget their original unity. Correspondingly, the tale runs on three planes which are separate from each other and are only joined together again after overcoming many difficulties:

- On one, there is the high plane of the royal castle where the king's son lives. He stands for the soul of the human being, for our angelic side which does not succumb to the rules of physical space and linear time. The king's son can also be understood as 'God's Son', a symbol for a person's all-embracing spiritual Self.

- On another plane, there is the family of Cinderella which is bound up with the fabric of earthly life and its limitations in time and space. The troubles which happen to the family symbolize the challenges which the Iron Age has placed before the human race.

- On the third plane, there is the organizational plane of principles which condition life as a whole. On the one hand, this concerns the God principle, symbolized by the father. Although it runs counter to the logic of separating the above-named planes, he appears as the sole father, as much so in his relationship to the king's son as to Cinderella. The dead mother on the other hand represents the Goddess principle which, in the name of the patriarchal domination which extends over the Iron Age, has been forced out of our consciousness.

The tale begins with the portent of the mother's death and the daughter's grief over her loss. Here the story is concerned with the threshold experience — expressed in the picture language of a fairy tale — which is imprinted on us at the beginning of the present phase of humankind's evolution. In order to grow up to be independent, a person must separate from that most marvelous sense of Oneness with the life streams of Earth in which, during the previous age, our development was happily embedded. It follows that the mother's death refers to a radical and tragic change in the history of the evolution of humankind, one which has led us forward into a phase of inward fragmentation.

In the fairy tale this phase is announced with the father's

decision to take a new wife into his house. However, the stepmother brings not one but two daughters with her into the family; in the language of fairy tales it is said of them that they are 'lovely and fair of face but nasty and black of heart'. Quite clearly, this represents a step away from unity and towards polarity. Polarity manifests itself in the distinction between the outer and the inner, the division into positive and negative, and in a pendulum movement between the material and the spiritual. The two newly arrived daughters symbolize the polarized picture of the world which, little by little, became people's primary paradigm after the withdrawal of the Goddess. The original cyclical *connection* with the wholeness of life — for which the Goddess stands — was replaced by a new psychic order which is characterized by the principle of *separation*.

In the picture language of the fairy tale this separation is expressed in the different status which contrasts Cinderella with the family's two step-sisters: Cinderella must get up early and light the fire; she must cook and wash the clothes and is even made to tie her step-sisters' shoes. The latter only look to getting out of their chores. Despite this they sleep in a white bed while Cinderella is nightly assigned to a place among the ashes in the hearth.

The depth of the inner division between spirit and soul to which people sink in the Iron Age becomes clear when the father asks all three daughters what gift he should bring them from the city. Corresponding to their egocentric ideals, the step-sisters want pretty clothes and jewelry. In contrast, Cinderella trusts in the wisdom of nature and asks her father for nothing more than the first hazel twig to knock against his hat on his way homeward.

In accordance with his promise, the father gives Cinderella a hazel twig, which, as befits a hazel twig, possesses magic powers. Cinderella sticks it in her mother's grave and waters it with her tears. From it grows a beautiful tree which showers her with everything which she asks her mother to give her. Transposed into linear understanding, this means that Cinderella stands for that part of the fragmented human which, though forced into the subconscious, still remains connected with the cycle of change from death to rebirth.

In order not to lose ourselves in the images of fairy tales, we should bear in mind that all the people who appear there represent the scattered pieces of the Being of humankind. The king's son, as already mentioned, symbolizes the eternal aspect of the human being, the soul-spiritual Self, which knows the cosmic rhythms of human evolution. It knows that the separation of the Being of humankind from the wholeness of life —which occurred in the course of the Iron Age — has now fulfilled its task. Individualization is concluded. Now changes are queuing up, the time for reconnection has come. The 'king's son' is looking for ways to bring together the splintered parts of the human being. In the language of the fairy tale, this means that he wishes to wed, and to find his true bride he will order three festival balls.

The father and mother stand respectively for the divine core of the human being and for the horizon within which human evolution is accomplished. Typically, the dead mother is replaced by the disastrous stepmother. She symbolizes the religious ideas, social norms and psychological patterns which, in the framework of the Iron Age, have slowly replaced the human being's loving and universal relationship with life and its several dimensions. People today seek to know truth through these sorts of artificial masks and filters instead of resonating in direct oneness with the wholeness of life. Instead of finding it, they become ever more fragmented and robbed of their wholeness.

The results of this self-alienation are represented by the two step-sisters. They represent the partial aspect of the self, split off and becoming independent, which in modern man is designated as Ego. Just as the two step-sisters, who are

wholly given over to outward appearances and glamour, rule over Cinderella's house, so the external I — the Ego — rules over the thoughts and actions of the Iron Age person. The problem is that the Ego, entangled in its one-sidedness and superficiality, is incapable of providing a person with stability, and groundedness and a foundation in the spiritual soul. In consequence it waivers between belief and doubt, between hate and love, between enthusiasm for the spiritual and abandonment to the material.

Only the true Self can ensure a person psychological stability, groundedness and a soul-spiritual foundation, and this has been overlooked and forced onto the plane of the subconscious. In the fairy tale this repressed Self bears the name of Cinderella. Instead of being able to sleep in the bed of social acceptance, Cinderella must satisfy herself with sleeping among the ashes, hence her name. The ashes represent what is left over from the fire which once shone brightly, visible to everyone. Cinderella stands for the Self which, banished to a person's subconscious, still pursues from there the process of their independent evolution.

Referring now to human history, I equate the 'king son's' invitation to the dance with the momentous event of Jesus' revelation of Christ at the beginning of our era. I do so because the dance will reconnect the fragmented parts of humankind. One can view Jesus as one whose works and teaching called on the isolated parts of the human being and pointed to the necessary process by which they could find themselves together again. For example, one of Jesus' statements speaks simply but precisely to the 'Cinderella complex', i.e., about a person's Self being forced into the subconscious: "Is a lamp brought in to be put under a tub or under the bed? Surely to be put on the lamp-stand? For there is nothing hidden, but it must be disclosed, nothing kept secret except to be brought to light. Anyone who has ears for listening should listen!" (Mark 4:21).

However, the turnaround from repression of the person-

al light to its recognition — let us call it the true Self —
cannot be accomplished on the plane of the intellect, but
only through a change process. Jesus indicates this in
extremely abbreviated form: "For there is nothing hidden,
but it must be disclosed, nothing kept secret except to be
brought to light."

What once represented bliss for the human being, the
light of their Self, must first experience denial and repression so that it may be drawn within. The fire must be taken
within in order to experience a refinement by soul and spirit. What appears outwardly as a phase of repression has a
positive side on its reverse. A person is forced to practice
humility, to ask ever and again about the meaning of their
life, and must learn to discriminate between what is useful
for life and what is not. In this way the individual slowly
matures to the point of discovering their hidden light, and
in the final phase of the process, lets it shine on the outside.
The light of the Self is now clear and sufficiently conscious
'to be put on the lamp-stand'.

By means of a parable, Jesus emphasizes that the evolving human must unavoidably go through this change
process before the due time arrives for the reconnection of
the fragmented parts of their being. This parable is about
the ten young women who took their lamps and went to
meet the bridegroom:

"Then the kingdom of Heaven will be like this: Ten
wedding attendants took their lamps and went to meet the
bridegroom. Five of them were foolish and five were sensible: the foolish ones, though they took their lamps, took no
oil with them, whereas the sensible ones took flasks of oil as
well as their lamps. The bridegroom was late, and they all
grew drowsy and fell asleep. But at midnight there was a
cry, 'Look! The bridegroom! Go out and meet him.' Then
all those wedding attendants woke up and trimmed their
lamps, and the foolish ones said to the sensible ones, 'Give
us some of your oil: our lamps are going out.' But they

replied, 'There may not be enough for us and for you; you had better go to those who sell it and buy some for yourselves.' They had gone off to buy it when the bridegroom arrived. Those who were ready went in with him to the wedding hall and the door was closed. The other attendants arrived later. 'Lord, Lord,' they said, 'open the door for us.' But he replied, 'In truth I tell you, I do not know you.'" (Mat 25).

This parable is also about the repressed Self, like the lamp placed under the tub — and corresponds to the image of Cinderella. In this story however it is the oil which plays the role of key symbol. The lamps cannot be lit at the decisive moment unless the oil is properly prepared. In other words, we cannot underestimate the importance of the Cinderella phase of our development. It is the phase when, unnoticed on the outside, the seeds of our future and further development are planted. The humiliations, pressures and tests which a person undergoes in this phase make it possible for them to reach the stage of clarity necessary for the reconnection with one's own divine Self. The parable ends with a warning that the fateful moment of the imminent marriage with one's 'Higher Self' can pass a person by if they have slept through the preparation phase.

In the Cinderella story, two tests symbolize the tasks which correspond to the period of the wedding preparations. She must pass these tests so that she can go to the festival balls which the king's son is holding to find the bride he longs for.

The tests demand that Cinderella sort through the ashes for the peas and lentils which the stepmother has thrown there. Translated, this means that during the preparation period a person must learn to distinguish the life-promoting seeds of their microcosm from the dead leftovers of the past. The seeds stand for the one, the ashes for the other. The Spirit of the Iron Age[1], incarnated through the stepmother, has deliberately made a chaos out of the inward parts of the human being — mixing the seeds with the ashes — to obstruct our development.

Cinderella could only complete her task on time because she had retained her connection with the wholeness of life's processes. To her help came three sorts of birds: two white doves, some turtle doves and 'all the birds of heaven'. These stand for the three different powers which are ready by their nature to assist the human being as the 'son/daughter of the Earth Goddess'. Their help is only granted us, however, if we admit into ourselves the inner wisdom of Earth and Nature and cherish it. The two white doves stand for the feminine spiritual power — also called Sophia, the Wisdom from the Archetypal Beginning, — the turtle doves for the forces of feeling and the birds of heaven for the intuition.

Modern man despises his feminine qualities — wisdom, powers of feeling and intuition — and therefore does not recognize when the time is ripe to reconnect his being with his Higher Self. His attitude was criticized by Jesus in the following words:

"When you see a cloud looming up in the West you say at once that rain is coming, and so it does. And when the wind is from the south you say it's going to be hot, and so it is. Hypocrites! You know how to interpret the face of the Earth and the sky. How is it that you do not know how to interpret these times?" (Luke 12:54).

However, neither was the process of reconnection a simple one from the perspective of the king's son. When he sent out invitations to the three festival balls, the bride he sought — Cinderella — was not officially allowed to take part because of prohibitions laid down by social and psychological norms. The true Self must remain at home although she had completed the tests imposed upon her. What is publicly offered to the king's son is the superficial Ego, incarnated in the two-stepsisters.

---

1 In Hindu tradition the Iron Age is described as 'Kali Yug' — the Age of the Black Goddess Kali.

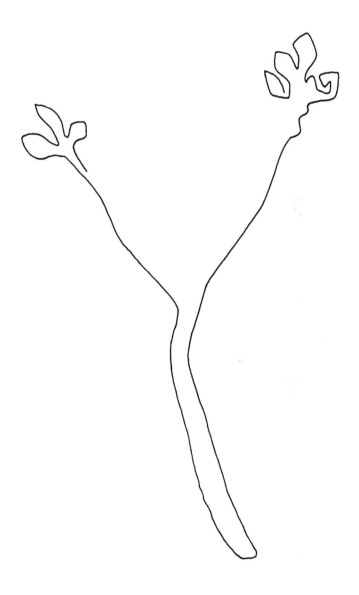

According to the cosmic clock whose rhythms bring to fruition the evolution of the human race, the time is ripe for our reconnection into a new unity — a new covenant with God. This means that the true bride cannot be prevented from taking part in the three festival balls. She enters each one secretly, covered in a robe woven of moonlight and sunshine given her by the tree of transformation which she herself had planted and cherished on her mother's grave. Clad in these garments of the spirit, she is invisible to her stepmother and stepsisters, but for the king's son she is unmistakable.

He recognizes his true bride at first glance, but circumstances are not ripe to enter into an enduring relationship. First the son must clear a path to their re-union and with his ax hew down the hurdles which bar the way to her. The first hurdle is a dovecote, the second a pear tree. These are temporary places of refuge for Cinderella after she has fled from the ball in order not to be recognized by her stepmother and stepsisters.

The dovecote stands for the fickle emotional qualities which distinguish our modern relationship to nature. It is a sort of love for living things, but one which lacks depth. It is deficient because there is no free, consciously taken decision to love earth and nature in their own being, rather than in relationship to humans, nor is there a willingness to recognize them in their several dimensions.

After the second ball Cinderella flees to the pear tree which is heavy with fruit. This tree stands as the symbol for the vital forces of earth which, if they are abused, can be a barrier on the evolutionary path of humankind and the planet. This addresses the danger presented by our culture's one-sided demands on the fertitlity and material riches of the Earth, which we extract by all possible means. The relationship with the spiritual and vital-energetic 'fruitfulness' of earth's systems is consequently denied and even impeded. The king's son — Christ — cuts down the pear tree as

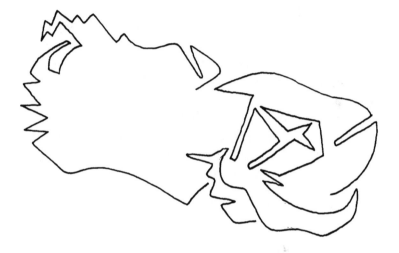

a sign that the one-sided hype of the earth's fruitfulness is an obstacle to the process of earth changes and human evolution.

At the third ball the king's son lays a trap for his still unrecognized bride. He causes black pitch to be smeared on the steps over which, on each previous occasion, she has fled away. When for the third time the fair one tears away from him and flees to reach her place among the ashes in good time, she loses her golden dancing shoe. It stays stuck to the pitch. At last the Prince has his hand on the key with which he can find his true bride.

This introduces the concluding phase of the reconnection of the separated parts of the human being. The barriers have been broken down and consequently the spiritual Self can become 'more deeply incarnated', that is to say enter into a closer connection with the earthly self. In the fairy tale it is told that the king's son now comes down from his castle and appears unexpectedly in the 'earthly family'. He lets his will be known: "She, whom this golden shoe fits, will be my wife."

The stepmother, representative of the ruling social and cultural norms, believes that the king's son has come to wed one of her two daughters — the Ego. She takes the elder to his side. In vain she tries to slip on the shoe. Her big toe is too large. On her mother's advice she cuts a piece off. But the deception is discovered while the king's son is riding with her to the castle: blood drips out of the golden shoe. The same sort of thing happens to her younger sister who cuts off her heel so that her foot may slip into the golden shoe.

The shoe is imprinted with the particular measure of the individual person, i.e., their personal seal, and stands for the archetypal pattern of the personal identity. This archetypal pattern, vibrating in the storehouse of earth's memory, provides the framework for a person's current incarnation. Stored in a deep layer of the earth, which I call the 'sub-elemental world'[2], this archetypal pattern ensures the uniqueness of every human being from incarnation to incarnation. It is through this archetypal pattern that a person comes into relationship with the wholeness of earth's systems — with Mother Earth. It represents the person's divine Self, contrasting with the earthly pole of human identity, and is therefore described as golden.

After the Prince has recognized the second bride as false and sent her back, he asks the father whether he does not have a third daughter. To be honest, the father must allow that there is still a Cinderella in the house. Admittedly, he calls her the 'nasty little Cinderella who cannot possibly be the bride.' The king's son insists on the test however, and behold, the golden shoe fits Cinderella as if she were poured into it. As the bride, she is now led home to the king's castle.

Let us look at this process in the mirror of the evolutionary history of humankind. Over the course of the last few millennia we have distanced ourselves more and more from the subtle foundations of life and the consciousness layers of earth, and have slowly lost our relationship with the archetypal pattern (see the definition in the third chapter) which guides the life of earth and preserves it in its several dimensional paths. The energetic, emotional and spiritual groundedness of the human being is to a large extent lost, although as incarnated humans we belong wholly to the life of earth.

The person who has lost their conscious connection with earth's wholeness is confined to the split-off portion which is represented by the Ego-aspect in the living human being. In consequence the golden shoe does not fit them, as demonstrated by the example of Cinderella's two stepsisters. It helps them not a bit to fake their relationship with earth, just as it does not help modern civilization to

---

2 See my book *Healing the Heart of the Earth*, p.125.

take an approach to the solution of ecological problems which is apparently earth-oriented but actually materialistic. We can certainly claim, more than any culture before us, to have penetrated the substance of earthly matter, and we persistently work with material things. Unfortunately these are only the thinnest, most external layers of the Earth Being, the largest and most important part of whom — like Cinderella — remains overlooked and despised. By this I am thinking of the vital-energetic organism of Earth, her planes of intelligence and feeling and her divine essence. As soon as our groundedness is put to the test — when we have to try on the 'shoe', an action necessary to reconnect the split-off portion — the tragic fact is revealed that actually for the earth we are already dead. It does not suffice to cut off a big toe from the front or a heel from behind.

However, in no way should we understand the message of the Cinderella story as meaning that the Son of God will come and separate those people who have lost their connection with the Earth Mother from those who have remained true! We should remember that every person who comes into a fairy tale represents different parts of one and the same human being, even those parts which have become alienated and hostile to each other. In consequence, no one can be cursed and cut off without the one who speaks the curse being themselves cursed and crippled.

The statement contained in the story is aimed rather at making people aware of the key significance of their 'Cinderella' for their future development. In the one-sided perspective of the Iron Age, the relationship with the Earth Mother is suppressed and made ever more taboo. Finally, it is only allowed to dwell in the shadow realm of our subconscious. Its powers are declared useless for the building of our culture, and it is cast onto the rubbish heap of the subconscious.

But, woe, oh woe! When our development arrives at the phase when the human being is to be reconnected — Jesus

describes it as the phase of the Son of Man — then things will become difficult. The reconnection between the 'angelic human' and the 'earthly human' in us can only be accomplished when it is based on the archetypal pattern where their belonging together has been encoded since the beginning of creation. If a person's relationship to this archetypal pattern has deteriorated, then the future fusion of their being is only possible if they awaken from their alienation in good time and choose their 'Cinderella' as the cornerstone of their new identity.

'Cornerstone' is an allusion to the well-known words of Jesus which are documented in all four gospels: "Jesus said, 'Show me the stone which the builders have rejected. That one is the cornerstone.'" (Tm, Log. 66)

In Luke's gospel the same statement is repeated in the form of Jesus quoting from a biblical psalm: "Then what does this text in the scriptures mean: The stone which the builders rejected has become the cornerstone?" To this he added the following words which point towards an inexorable decision: "Anyone who falls on that stone will be dashed to pieces; anyone it falls on will be crushed." (Luke 20:17)

When I read that added sentence for the first time, I must admit that I doubted its authenticity. However, despite the content which makes it sound so merciless, it displays a healthy etheric structure. So I thought to myself that two of Jesus' sayings, each of which is true in itself, may have been wrongly coupled together. Finally, after a more precise reading of the conclusion of the Cinderella story, I could understand the addition.

When the king's son was leading the rightful bride — that is to say 'the rejected cornerstone' — home to her wedding, two doves settled on her shoulders. One sat upon her left, the other upon her right shoulder, as befits the daughter of the Archetypal Goddess. The two stepsisters also accompanied her to the wedding, the elder to her right and

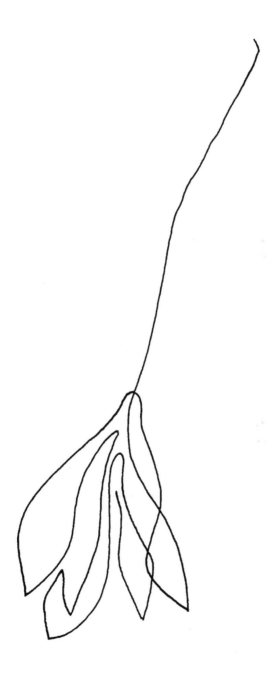

the younger to her left. As they went, the doves pecked out an eye from each of them. On the return from the wedding their places were reversed, the younger being on the right and the elder on the left. And the doves pecked out their second eye too. And so the blind ones were blinded, which is a way of emphasizing their one-sided way of looking at things.

It must however be said that neither in the fairy tale nor in Jesus' statement is any act of revenge intended. The dashing to pieces and crushing of the duality, and the blinding of the right and the left eyes respectively, symbolize the obliteration of the partial aspect of the human being which we call 'Ego'. This was split off and now is integrated into the Wholeness of the Self; it renders service and belongs to our 'Cinderella Self' who is resurrected like a phoenix from the ashes. After 'her light was put on the lamp-stand', Cinderella awakens to be a royal bride.

Chapter 14

Humanity in the Mirror
of the Present Earth Changes

The dramatic impact of the processes leading to the reconnection of the separated parts of the Being of humanity is
perhaps to be felt at its strongest in a conversation between
Jesus the Master and his disciples:

"(They saw) a Samaritan carrying a lamb on his way to
Judea. He said to his disciples, '(Why does) that man
(carry) the lamb around?' They said to Him, 'So that he
may kill it and eat it.' He said to them, 'While it is alive, he
will not eat it, but only when he has killed it and it has
become a corpse.' They said to Him, 'He cannot do otherwise.' He said to them, 'You too, look for a place for yourselves within Repose, lest you become a corpse and be
eaten.' (Tm, Log. 60)

This conversation is taken from the Gospel of Thomas
which was found translated into the Coptic language. It is
questionable whether the modern translation into English
is really so unambiguous that it should be left exclusively as
worded above. The decisive point of the conversation,
where Jesus gives instruction how to avoid the danger of the
'spiritual death', is for example rendered differently in
another English translation[1]: "You too seek for yourselves a
place within for rest, so that you will not become a corpse

1 Robert M. Grant with David Noel Freedman: *The Secret Sayings of Jesus
according to the Gospel of Thomas.*

and be eaten."

In the context of those aspects of Jesus' teaching which are devoted to a person's self-knowledge, we can identify the 'place of rest within' as the communal Self of humanity which at the present time has been forced into the subconscious. We recognized it as the 'Cinderella-Self' when we considered the story of Cinderella in the previous chapter. We need to seek for this misjudged Self so that the process of reconnecting the splintered parts of the Being of humanity does not find us unprepared, as happened to Cinderella's stepsisters.

In contrast, the Gospel according to Matthew offers a completely different solution to this problem confronting humankind on the threshold of the 21st century. As an alternative to reconnecting our estranged parts through an inner process, we are offered a solution 'from outside' — the 'Second Coming' of Christ in the form of the Last Judgment:

"When the Son of man comes in his glory, escorted by all the angels, then he will take his seat on his throne of glory. All nations will be assembled before him and he will separate people one from another as the shepherd separates sheep from goats. He will place the sheep on his right hand and the goats on his left. Then the King will say to those on his right hand, 'Come, you whom my Father has blessed, take as your heritage the kingdom prepared for you since the foundation of the world...Then he will say to those on his left hand, 'Go away from me, with your curse upon you, to the eternal fire prepared for the devil and his angels.'" (Mat 25:31, 41)

When I contemplate the four etheric layers of this section of text, I find an extreme confusion such as I have never seen anywhere else in the gospels. The earth ether, which should lie very close to the rows of letters, has been driven into the heights. In contrast, the air element, which should be high above, lies deep below on the lines of text.

Adding to the distortion, the fire ether rises far too high, as if blown by a bellows. It is to be sensed in the place which the air ether normally occupies. The water ether feels extremely turbulent. Its layer lies underneath the earth ether, representing a further distortion. This is very far from the usual pattern of the four ethers found in the gospel texts.

The dramatic but confused etheric structure of the text of the Last Judgment is unmistakable evidence that its core contains a fiery and portentous statement which, however, has been misinterpreted and misunderstood. Because of it we have come to the idea of a Hereafter at 'the end of time', when the good would be divided from the bad. It is worth noting that this is only to be found in the Gospel according to Matthew, which is deeply involved in the ideology of dualism, as has been pointed out several times already.

My feeling is that the idea of the Last Judgment was kindled by a group of Jesus' sayings which have future events and developments as their theme. Among them we find statements which relate to the destruction of Jerusalem by the Roman legions in the year 70 of our era. These are indicated by the words, "Before this generation has passed away, all these things will have taken place,"[2] and are of lesser interest to us today.

However, there are others of Jesus' sayings which do relate to the epochal change affecting humankind which is at last approaching its critical point in our own day. The sayings suggest that at the appropriate time this critical point would be recognized as a kind of rebirth of humanity and be associated with the concept of the 'Coming of the Son of Man'. To these belong the following three sayings:

1 "Take the fig tree as a parable: as soon as its twigs grow supple and its leaves come out, you know that summer is

---

2 Unfortunately in the process of the consolidation of the gospels, the relationship between this sentence and the events to which it refers was lost.

near. (So with you when you see all these things: know that he is near, right at the gates.)" (Mat 24:32; the parentheses are inserted by me because the relevant sentence is strongly impressed with the author's intention to use it to prepare for the idea of the Last Judgment.)

2 "As it was in Noah's day, so will it be when the Son of man comes. For in those days before the Flood people were eating, drinking, taking wives, taking husbands, right up to the day Noah went into the ark, and they suspected nothing till the Flood came and swept them all away. This is what it will be like when the Son of man comes." (Mat 24:37)

3 "There will be signs in the sun and moon and stars; on earth nations in agony, bewildered by the turmoil of the ocean and its waves; men fainting away with terror and fear at what menaces the world, for the powers of heaven will be shaken. And then they will see the Son of man coming in a cloud with power and great glory. (Luke 21:25)

These three sayings in which Jesus refers to future events have in common the concept that the rebirth of humanity is connected with changes in Nature and inconceivable alterations in the earth's surface and surrounding cosmos. It is worth noting that the approach of that time is symbolized by the changes in the fig tree 'whose twigs grow supple and leaves come out'. As discussed in Chapter 8, the fig tree stands as a symbol for the life power of Earth.

In the second statement Jesus warns that the changes would be so subtle that people, who are so busy living according to their old ideas, will not even be in a position to notice the changes taking place around them and in themselves. He refers to the memory of Noah and the Flood, which according to traditions in many cultures overtook the earth in some long-ago time. The wave of changes on the earth's surface may then have been so powerful that the only survivors — symbolized by Noah and his ark — were those who were alert enough to interpret the signs of the time. That enabled them to attune to the changes in good time, so that — figuratively speaking — they could proceed in common with the Earth organism to a new plane of existence.

The most impressive warning that this change in the Earth organism is now in progress is one which I experienced on November 4, 1997. It began with a dream in which I was running crazily among people who, deeply immersed in their own concerns, were walking in all possible directions across a spacious town square. I was running to and fro and all the time crying out with all my might, "Don't ever think that reality now is what it once was; that is no longer true. What we're seeing now is only a memory of it." The very volume of my cries awakened me. What astounded me then, apart from the precise nature of the statement, was the language I had used. I was sleeping at home in Slovenia and yet I shouted the momentous sentences not in Slovenian but in German. It could be a sign that this was not about a local matter, but was something which concerned all of us.

As soon as I was awake, I got up and immediately took myself out into the surrounding countryside to perceive what possible changes had occurred. Now I was really amazed. My method of assessing the general quality of the earth organism in a particular place consists of touching into the radiation coming from the ground, a simple gesture which can be carried out quickly and almost unnoticed in every spot. I bend down to the earth and with my left hand reach into the radiation from the ground. Then I let my hand glide freely upwards with the 'up-draft' of the ground radiation and in so doing observe what sort of quality is affecting the hand, how high it is being carried and in

---

3 See further in my book, *Schule der Geomantie*, Section 2.3.A.

what type of motion. For years now I have been gathering experience with this simple method of testing[3].

When I tested the radiation from the earth floor on that early morning, I was astounded: the radiation field had tilted 180 degrees! The radiation which up till then I had felt as rising from the ground now felt as if it was beaming downwards from the earth's surface, in the direction of the earth's interior. I also reached out in contemplation to a number of power points and all were overturned. For example, the force-columns of an important irradiation point appeared to have been replaced by a hole which led deep inside the earth.

Concerned that, in view of this ecological disequilibrium, the prophecies about the tilting of the earth's axis might have been fulfilled, I asked my colleague Ana Pogacnik to request the help of Devos, the Angel of Earth Healing who has already been mentioned. He reassured us while explaining that the geomantic systems of the place had tilted because the Earth had gone through a deep change in her organism. As a result the most sensitive power points in our neighborhood had turned upside-down and this had detrimentally affected the whole force system of the place. Devos gave us specific instructions how we could bring the situation back into its normal paths by using a type of 'acupuncture singing'[4].

Although the event left behind no untoward consequences, the angel's casual mention of presently occurring earth changes made me sit up and review matters. First, during the previous months I had noticed fluctuations in the force systems of earth which I could not bring into a state of order. Second, it struck me that since August 1997 there had been no assaults on the part of the contrary powers, such as myself and my family had been uninterruptedly exposed to beforehand. Since then, everything which we

4 See further in my book, *Healing the Heart of the Earth*, p. 168.

228 *Christ Power and the Earth Goddess*

perceive as impediments have functioned only to remind us that the old thought patterns wish to be dissolved and the only concern at present is to forgive ourselves and others.

All of this was sufficient reason to request Ana to ask the Devos, the Angel of Earth Healing, for more detail about the present earth changes. The message, which Ana wrote down on December 22, 1997, began with the words:

The Earth also has its own evolution, and this again is connected with your evolution and with ours. One could even say that her evolution is extensively dependent on both our and yours. This matter concerns an energetic and etheric evolution and the evolution of various intelligences which are connected with Earth, and so on. In any case, it concerns an evolution in several layers which is very complex.

Through your tendency towards individual evolution, you human beings have so totally 'swamped' everything around you that it is beginning to restrict Earth's own evolution and in a certain way throttle it. Through your capacity to give your whole attention and all your forces to your own evolution, you humans have developed a most impressive dominance. I would not like to say that it was wrong of you to develop yourselves and grow ever stronger. It is quite right, as long as in doing so you do not 'push others to the wall.'

You are not sufficiently aware how important this planet is for you. Actually you are a part of it — at least you ought to be. Instead of that you try to take Earth's strength away from her, although in so doing you would bring to nothing your own evolution and your own essence which she is carrying. You think your goal is to take over the ruling role and grasp the tiller in your hand. However that is not possible for

*you. Taken all together as humankind, you are cer-
tainly strong but inwardly too much divided to be
able to dispose of a correspondingly broad vision and
a sufficiently ramified energy. Another impediment is
the fact that the only real possibility and the only constructive resolution for your evolution lies in the connection between you, the Earth and ourselves (the
angelic world). Only by joining the three evolutions
together are all the necessary elements and forces
included. What is needed here is a symbiosis and a
bonding of each with the other, so that a unique
Wholeness comes into being.*

In the further course of the message, the Angel of Earth
Healing went into detail about the individual characteris-
tics of all three evolutions, giving particular consideration
to humanity's place between the world of angels and the
world of earth. He allowed that we are the active element
within this triangle, which does not mean however that we
are independent of our two evolutionary partners. In any
case, it is these two partners which make our active role
possible.

Devos also confirmed that the further evolution of the
wholeness of life, as it exists today, is extensively dependent
on human beings. We have developed our free will and our
reason and so have the capacity to decide independently
how far we are ready to participate in the further evolution
of our universe.

Illustrating the importance of the human role between
the two evolutions is the fact, among others, that the angelic world can only collaborate in the processes of the earth
changes to the extent that we make it possible for them to
do so. Devos emphasized that the angels are certainly free
to be creative on the plane of their own world, but they are
not able to work under the conditions imposed by matter.
That is only possible for them through the mediating role
of human beings.

Another reason why the further evolution of Earth is extremely dependent on human beings is that we are so deeply interwoven with the fabric of her life. The Angel of Earth Healing clarified our actual situation in relationship to Earth in the following way:

> *You have reached the point where you can take no more from Earth. You have exhausted her too severely. You must learn to begin a mutual exchange where giving and taking are equal. Then nothing will ever be lacking. Give love and you will experience still more love. Your role in relationship to Earth is similar to your relationship to us.*

In the further course of the message Devos explained that at specific phases of their development all three evolutions reach points where a decision must be made on how to proceed further. This is as true for a person's own path of development as it is for the path of humanity as a whole, and it is true also for planet Earth. In very occasional cases it happens that different evolutions arrive simultaneously at such a focal point where decisions must be taken about the future. One can then speak of a highly important moment of decision.

According to the Angel of Earth Healing, we are right now approaching such a point which has a determining significance for humanity, the earth and the angelic world. He confirms that this moment is decisive for each one of the three evolutions and therefore for the wholeness of the worlds which together we are forming. Then he continues:

> *Thus, our concern is with a general decision which, however, has already been in preparation for a long time. We are actually dealing with a transition to a new plane, which is only possible in stages and after a long prepara-tory period.*
>
> *Too often I have emphasized that life is made possible only by an evolution which leads it forward.*

Otherwise it loses its meaning and purpose. This present transition is also a furtherance of your path. If all human beings were ready to cooperate, then it could happen in stages and the ascent to the next stage would be easy. Otherwise this transition can become very painful. That is of special concern to you human beings because you are in a corporeal body and least able to adapt.

Above all, it is necessary that all should work together to make this transition, otherwise there is no chance that evolution will be continued in the form of the wholeness of the world as they exist today.

Devos tried to provide more information about what, as a practical matter, is happening as regards the current earth changes. First, there is a change in the quality of earth forces. This makes possible the further development of the structural field of earth forces, which in turn instigates the further perfecting of its force systems. In consequence, the energies of the planet will become fundamentally stronger.

The second concern is with the way the forces of earth are perceived and applied:

Energy will be recognized as the life force, as life itself, as the love which we all share with each other. We are all suffused with it. Through this we will become a Wholeness, we will become One.

This message, which Ana received on the darkest day of the year, sounds optimistic about our common future. It also indicates briefly what actions we humans can personally take to ensure that the earth changes will have a positive outcome. The Angel of Earth Healing encourages us, "to consciously carry out certain alterations," so as to change ourselves:

I would not like to lay too heavy a burden on you. I should like to confirm how important you are and what an important role you play in the general evo-

lution, whose witnesses you are. Be aware of that and rejoice over it.

It is necessary that, to a certain degree, you collaborate concretely in the transition I have described and consciously implement certain alterations. Nonetheless, the development (of the transition) is already so well prepared that you might say that it is running of itself. It is indeed the result of a long preparatory phase which is leading to the alterations described.

The confidence of the Angel of Earth Healing in the constructive role of human beings may astonish us when we look around and see the accumulation of political, social and ecological problems with which we burden our world. We have therefore inclined toward a belief that in a critical moment God and the Earth could lose patience and strike out with catastrophes.

In so thinking we are not aware that when we cherish such thoughts and fears, we are moving only on the flat plane of reason and from this level can perceive but a thin layer of reality. In contrast, an angel's vision is several dimensional and in no way limited to the surface of the soap bubble which we know as our world.

What we know as our normal world is actually a construct created so that over the course of millennia humanity could work out its evolution. Like all artificial structures, the world has its purpose which, at some time or other, will be fulfilled. If it has fulfilled its task and cannot encourage evolution any further, such a world structure becomes a hindrance to the path of development and a monstrous burden for Earth. It is then time to burst the soap bubble.

The difficulty is that the majority of people have lost the instinct for recognizing the several layers of Earth, and also the several dimensions of their own being. They identify themselves with the one-dimensional world-structure, which, taken by itself, has no quality of life but was 'constructed' for the preservation and promotion of human evolution. Within this structure the strength of earth's systems was to a large extent muted and filtered so that humans should have an environment where they were forced to develop their independence and creativity if they wished to survive. If this filtering structure has now fulfilled its task and is being dissolved, it does not mean that earth's systems collapse. It only appears that the end of the world is in progress because of our unfortunate identification with the space-time structure which is at present being dismantled.

Jesus gave timely warnings about identification with the transitory structure of the world. Here are two examples from the Gospel of Thomas: "Jesus said, 'Whoever has come to understand the world has found (only) a corpse, and whoever has found a corpse is superior to the world.'" (Tm, Log. 56). The meaning is reinforced in this second saying of Jesus: "(Jesus said,) 'If you do not fast as regards the world, you will not find the Kingdom.'" (Tm, Log. 27)

It is obvious that Jesus was contrasting the concept of a one-dimensional world-structure with the vision of a living kingdom of heaven which unites the forces of Earth and Spirit in their several dimensionalities and can therefore ensure eternal life. In a further statement, reported by the evangelists Matthew and Luke, Jesus provides the key which enables us to release ourselves from the false identification with the 'soap bubble' world: "Get yourselves purses that do not wear out, treasure that will not fail you, in heaven where no thief can reach it and no moth destroy it. For wherever your treasure is, that is where your heart will be too." (Luke 12:33)

The heart is to be seen as a symbol for a person's identity; in my heart, I am who I am. If we let ourselves consider how to withdraw our attention from the world of appearances, where the 'the thieves rule and the moths devour', and instead live life in its several dimensions, then we will experience a wonderful inner enrichment. Our own life will become several dimensional and fulfilled with joy. In the same moment that we begin to identify with this 'treasure', we have freed ourselves from the dreaded end of the world. When it actually becomes necessary to dismantle the outdated world-structure, we will suffer no harm. Our being is not in the world but is grounded in the reality of life.

There was a further powerful shift in the process of earth changes on February 10, 1998, the day of the full moon. To be honest, I was not prepared for it. I had been shaken awake by some illogical tremors, and finally went out into the moonlight to sense the earth radiations and feel how things stood with them. A new surprise awaited me. The radiations emanating from the ground were fundamentally altered. They had taken on a soft, watery, feminine character. Their characteristic pattern began to form itself in a half-bow deep in the earth, but then did not continue in an upward direction but instead glided horizontally to and fro, as if someone was stroking a watery surface. At first I thought that the new form of earth radiation might be the effect of the full moon. However, it did not change when the moon waned. After a few days I also noticed a clear differentiation. In general, the ground radiation had retained the new, watery quality. However, in specific places there are force fields which looked like islands of radiation. These islands always display one and the same vibrational pattern. I experience it such that my outstretched hand begins to turn into a slow, solemn rhythm until it has described a complete circle. It is describing a cosmogram of perfection!

These were reasons enough to question the Angel of Earth Healing once again about the actual status of the earth changes. His message, which Ana received on February 15, 1998, begins with the words:

We find ourselves in the epoch where the greatest changes are taking place; you are a part of them, just as are we and the earth. We are taking part in a united evolution which we can only go through together; only together are we strong enough for it, and only together do we represent a Wholeness.

The changes are manifesting on all planes. You will take part in them personally; they will be felt by humankind and by civilization... In this we too are experiencing an evolution and are growing together with you. Nonetheless, the changes will also be obvious in the earth, since it has an important role to play in the transition.

What you yourself have determined, and what Marko has perceived, are the expression of these changes. Because we have already accomplished much together on the path toward this evolution, greater disruptions are not necessary. Yet there are changes which are still necessary. What you are experiencing, and what I am talking about, is only a phase of the development.

What you have felt as the watery element is a strong Yin element which at the same time expresses the manner in which the energy streams and vibrates in wave form... This is only one phase in the formation of another vibration of earth, a higher layer of force which will develop over time and offer a parallel to earth's existing force-system. It will make possible the several dimensionalities of life.

In the further course of the message, the Angel of Earth Healing gave details about the particular vibrational qualities of the individual sacred places which I have mentioned before. He confirmed that particular places and points on the earth's surface, those which are sufficiently pure and

236   Christ Power and the Earth Goddess

strong and on that account capable of vibrating on a higher frequency plane, have undertaken a sort of mediating function within the change process. It is their function to prevent the existing force-system from breaking apart. After all, it is this system which is providing the foundation on which the new layers are constructed. Many of these places worldwide, Devos added in praise, were prepared for this task during the last few years by individual groups engaged in earth healing work.

And what is the state of the mysteriously woven relationship between human beings and the angelic kingdom? The messages of the Angel of Earth Healing emphasize over and over again that in respect to the relationships between humans and Earth, the third partner, the world of angels, must not be forgotten. What does Jesus have to say about this? We find an instance in the parable of the unjust steward: "He also said to his disciples, 'There was a rich man and he had a steward who was denounced to him for being wasteful with his property. He called for the man and said, 'What is this I hear about you? Draw me up an account of your stewardship because you are not to be my steward any longer.' Then the steward said to himself, 'Now that my master is taking the stewardship from me, what am I to do? Dig? I am not strong enough. Go begging? I should be too ashamed. Ah, I know what I will do to make sure that when I am dismissed from office there will be some to welcome me into their homes.' Then he called his master's debtors one by one. To the first he said, 'How much do you owe my master?' 'One hundred measures of oil,' he said. The steward said, 'Here, take your bond; sit down and quickly write fifty.' To another he said, 'And you, sir, how much do you owe?' 'One hundred measures of wheat,' he said. The steward said, 'Here, take your bond and write eighty.' The master praised the dishonest steward for his astuteness. For the children of this world are more astute in dealing with their own kind than are the children of light." (Luke 16)

The role of the unjust steward stands for the human role on earth, because the Lord gave the stewardship of the earth to us. It is true that we have dealt badly with the earth. We have disturbed her equilibrium, reduced the variety of animal and plant species and harmed her vital-energetic systems. However it is also true that in so doing we have learned something which not even such an advanced evolution as the angels can claim: rationally, this means that we think and decide from our own individual sense of independence. It is this quality which is demonstrated by the example of the unjust steward, after he had learned that he would lose his position.

This is also the reason why the Lord speaks words of praise about human beings: "The children of this world are more astute in dealing with their own kind than are the children of light." We should not overlook the fact that this is not a value judgment, but a recognition of what, in conjunction with earth's systems, human beings have achieved "in dealing with their own kind."

These messages from the Angel of Earth Healing make it clear that now at the end of the 20th century we are not dealing with the human being as a sinner who must be punished. In the celebrated parable of the prodigal son Jesus has foreseen the happy outcome of the dramatic processes involved in human evolution. Instead of sorrow and chaos, the parable ends with rejoicing over the rebirth of humanity. (Luke 15:11)

The parable tells of a man who has two sons. The following words spoken by his father characterize the elder son as belonging to the angelic world: "My son, you are with me always and all I have is yours." Angels do not need to undergo the turbulence of personal experience for the purposes of their development. They remain from eternity to eternity as the perfect expression of the Divine. The Father says: "All I have is yours."

In contrast, the younger son, who stands for the evolution of humankind, desired his inheritance and after a few days "got together everything he had and left for a distant country." Here we are speaking of the human beings decision to walk on their own individual path of experience. It is further indicated that to be able to gather experiences and acquire knowledge, they must incarnate on earth — in "a distant country." The parable continues with a symbolic description of the phases through which they must pass, corresponding to the experiences of incarnation: "A few days later, the younger son got together everything he had and left for a distant country where he squandered his money on a life of debauchery. When he had spent it all, that country experienced a severe famine, and now he began to feel the pinch; so he hired himself out to one of the local inhabitants who put him on his farm to feed the pigs. And he would willingly have filled himself with the husks the pigs were eating but no one would let him have them. Then he came to his senses and said, 'How many of my father's hired men have all the food they want and more, and here am I dying of hunger! I will leave this place and go to my father and say: 'Father, I have sinned against heaven and against you; I no longer deserve to be called your son; treat me as one of your hired men.' So he left the place and went back to his father."

At this point the drama of the parable begins to unfold. It is the mirror image of the situation in which we find ourselves at this moment — cosmic moments can last for years. Human beings are so deeply immersed in matter and in the one-dimensional world that their only perspective is the desire to improve their actual situation. Figuratively speaking, so might a swineherd be so frantically hungry for the freedom of the spirit that he could imagine nothing better than to be the lowest servant in his father's house, simply to have enough to eat.

In light of the current earth changes, what then lay in the future is now here. The parable tries to give people the sense that this change concerns a quantum leap. Keeping to the language of the parable, his father will receive him with the highest honors as his reborn son. Even the ring, which in my dream of the Iron Age I had lost, is put back on his hand: "While he was still a long way off, his father saw him and was moved with pity. He ran to the boy, clasped him in his arms and kissed him. Then his son said, 'Father, I have sinned against heaven and against you. I no longer deserve to be called your son.' But the father said to his servants, 'Quick! Bring out the best robe and put it on him; put a ring on his finger and sandals on his feet. Bring the calf we have been fattening, and kill it; we will celebrate by having a feast, because this son of mine was dead and has come back to life; he was lost and is found.' And they began to celebrate."

Transposed to our present situation, whose circumstances appears to be anything but promising, the parable encourages us to believe wholeheartedly and in full consciousness that we have divine guidance on our path. When every single person has gone through the process of fundamental change — and the current earth changes are forcing all human beings to come to a decision in this regard — then we will participate in a new phase of evolution which the parable characterizes with such properties as wholeness, multi-dimensionality and joy.

However, it is not the parable's intention to make promises, but to confirm for us the meaningfulness of human evolution, sown though it is with difficulties. As difficult and painful as it may often be to walk on the path of change, it is a meaningful path. This conclusion follows from the comparison between the path of humanity and the path of angels, which is how the parable concludes: "Now the elder son was out in the fields, and on his way back, as he drew near the house, he could hear music and dancing. Calling one of the servants he asked what it was all about. The servant told him, 'Your brother has come, and your father has killed the calf we had been fattening because he has got him back safe and sound.' He was angry then and refused to go in, and his father came out and began to urge him to come in; but he retorted to his father, 'All these years I have slaved for you and never once disobeyed any orders of yours, yet you never offered me so much as a kid for me to celebrate with my friends. But, for this son of yours, when he comes back after swallowing up your property — he and his loose women — you kill the calf we had been fattening.' The father said, 'My son, you are with me always and all I have is yours. But it was only right we should celebrate and rejoice, because your brother here was dead and has come to life; he was lost and is found.'" (Luke 15:11-32)

The next shift in the earth changes happened shortly before the full moon on March 9, 1998. The radiation from the ground had changed again. Instead of being watery, a fiery quality has now come to expression. There followed a yet further change in the etheric aura of earth which took place in the night of April 19-20. The air element is now the predominant quality. In the following months the situation as regards earth radiation has remained unchanged. This means that a phase of the earth changes has been successfully resolved.

In this change process, the earth is going through the cycle of the different elemental qualities. The beginning point of the cycle was represented by the earth element, and there followed water and fire. Last came the turn of the air element, which is now to be felt as the predominant element[5].

My insight tells me that the earth changes have now moved onto other planes. What has remained stable are the above mentioned islands of light in the land- and cityscapes. Obviously these are ensuring that the life realms of the planet are not threatened by greater shocks during

5. See further on the theme of the predominant role of the air element in the future evolution of earth in my book *Nature Spirits & Elemental Beings*, p.173.

the current changes.

The question remains how we humans can best attune ourselves when the future earth changes become ever more clearly sensible. First of all, we should follow the example of the earth and nourish our inner place of repose. Just as the earth is creating islands of light to preserve her stability, so we should take care that under no circumstances do we lose our inner calm, that is, allow ourselves to be catapulted out of our heart center.

It makes sense to believe in the message of the parable of the son who was lost and found again, and not allow ourselves to be confused by 'false prophets'. Their catastrophe-oriented prophecies of earth changes arise from their limited insights into the mystery of the change and not from any overview of the necessary phases of the transition to a new stage of evolution.

We should turn towards nature, seek inner relationships with trees, rivers and localities ... Nature can never become separated from the circumstances of Earth. Therefore it offers the best chance of attuning oneself to what is happening with Earth at any given moment. For example, if one approaches a tree lovingly and lets oneself inwardly enter its presence, it will be happy to provide one with the feeling of how — beyond any illusion — reality is vibrating in that moment and in what direction the Earth is moving, taking with it the foundations of our life.

Do not worry! In the next thousand years there is time enough for every single human being to complete the processes of their evolution onto the step initiated by Jesus. Through its changes, Earth is there to create for us the circumstances which can best accelerate this process.

Chapter 15

*Contemplating Some
of the Sayings of Jesus*

The last two chapters described the processes of human evolution and raise the question, what can a person do in a practical way to consciously participate in them? Everything which Jesus said indicates that he did not intend to introduce a specific kind of spiritual discipline — something like Yoga. Rather he was teaching us to sanctify life just as it is. He spoke of a life which can have the quality of the kingdom of heaven provided the person awakens to his multi-dimensionality and knows how to handle his impulses sincerely and creatively.

Among some others of his sayings, this is made plain in his conversation with a Samaritan woman at a well. The woman asked Jesus whether people should pray to God on Mount Garizim — where their conversation took place — as did the Samaritans, or in Jerusalem as the Jews preferred. Jesus replied: "Believe me, woman, the hour is coming when you will worship the Father neither on this mountain nor in Jerusalem... But the hour is coming — indeed is already here — when true worshipers will worship the Father in spirit and truth: that is the kind of worshiper the Father seeks." (John 4:23)

I identify the expression "worship in spirit" as a way of sinking into one's heart center — I do not feel that the word 'meditation' is suitable, although it is currently used in this sense. To "worship in truth" I feel to be a synonym for 'worship in the fulfillment of one's daily life'. One of Jesus' statements from the Gospel of Thomas says something more precise to this effect: "His disciples questioned Him and said to Him, 'Do You want us to fast? How shall we pray? Shall we give alms? What diet shall we observe?' Jesus said, 'Do not tell lies, and do not do what you hate, for all things are plain in the sight of Heaven.'" (Tm, Log. 6)

In the following pages I have selected some of Jesus' sayings and put them into present-day speech in the hope that they will be of use to inform and enrich life choices. In order to recognize the multi-dimensionality of the sayings, I did not try to transpose them analytically but gave priority to the inner voice. Figuratively speaking, I have asked the modern instrument of consciousness which is the Christ Power within me to express in another way the same words that once were spoken.

Can any of you, however much you worry, add even a little period of time to the span of your life? (Luke 12:25)

The unfolding of the fabric of life makes it possible for all creatures to grow and develop. Worrying about the self creates a physical pressure which does not stand in a constructive relationship with the rhythmic weaving of life's fabric. Worry expresses one's fear of the unexpected happenings that life can bring; it is a way of fantasizing into life something which is not there.

Trust in the wisdom which is woven by the fabric of life. Even the knots in the fabric, tangled together out of difficulties, hide an opportunity to free oneself from old burdens, get to know an unrecognized side of one's being, get through a test... Trust in the wisdom woven by life's fabric and do not worry.

> *Whatever you have heard said in the dark will be
> heard in the daylight, and what you have whispered
> in each other's ear will be proclaimed from the house-
> tops. (Luke 12:3)*

A great change lies before us, and in part is already accomplished. What up till now we have experienced in the dark
of night while our consciousness is abroad in sleep, we will
in future be able to share in broad daylight. There will be
less and less of the strict division between our nightly experience of the spiritual plane and our experience of the material world during daylight consciousness. We will learn to
hear and understand in the light of day the things which
the soul could only tell us during sleep.

We will also learn to perceive and steadfastly maintain in
the great space of creation the quality of love which today
only circulates between people who love one another.
Figuratively speaking, that which we are accustomed 'to
whisper in each other's ear' will soon 'be proclaimed from
the housetops'. For all human beings, love will become a
sensible quality of space, recognized as the creative and
revivifying power of life.

> *Jesus said, "A grapevine has been planted outside of
> the Father, but being unsound, it will be pulled up by
> its roots and destroyed." (Tm, Log.40)*

Although it is true that there are some things which lie in
the realm of our own decision-making, and we can accomplish much by use of our own creative powers, it is unwise
to ignore the archetypal, spiritual ground of one's being and
so conduct ourselves as if we could grow by ourselves alone.

Beyond our independence, our being and doing is bound to eternity for it is there that 'our grapevine has been planted'. The misunderstanding arises because we are an individualized spark of eternity, and therefore the creative thrust of our being is directed towards individual evolution. Unavoidably, this leads us away from and out of the One Being which is the Whole.

Jesus' words warn us not to go ever further forward on the path towards individuation, or we shall forget the way back which joins us to our archetypal ground. That knowledge will be given us when we ask for it from our heart center.

Which of you here, intending to build a tower, would not first sit down and work out whether his resources are sufficient to complete it? Otherwise, it could happen that he lays the foundation and then finds himself unable to finish the work. And anyone who sees it would make fun of him and say, "Here is someone who began a building and was unable to finish it."
(Luke 14:28)

The path of life offers a person countless opportunities to evolve. Among them are some for which he or she is ready and strong and developed enough to seize hold of, play with them creatively and bring them into reality. But others also offer themselves which far exceed the person's powers or the knowledge they have acquired. It is wisdom to accept the first and reject the latter. Jesus warns us against taking on every challenge which at first glance appears possible and enticing, and then trying to make it happen. Some are only a test, to prove whether a person is sufficiently mature to decide what challenges they have grown strong enough, physically and spiritually, to cope with, and which are beyond them. The person who throws himself headlong into such life's temptations will find out sooner or later that he was not ready for them and "anyone who saw it would start making fun of him," because he had wanted to take on a project which, under the given circumstances, he could not bring to a conclusion.

If a woman has ten drachmas and loses one, does she not then light a lamp and sweep out the whole house and search tirelessly until she finds the coin? And when she had found it, she calls her friends and neighbors together, saying to them, "Rejoice with me, I have found the drachma which I lost." (Luke 15:8)

We humans bring with us all the things which we seek to acquire on our path through life. We are born from perfection, and everything, down to the last drachma, is given us to take with us on our way.

Personal development is not about finding something new, but about becoming conscious of what we already are and making that real in our lives. Thus it is that Jesus says that the woman already possessed the ten drachmas — the number of perfection — before she lost one of them. The lost drachma indicates a treasure which we despise and therefore have forced into the subconscious. The loss, whether it be of health, prosperity, love … — forces us to a fundamental 'house-cleaning', which means creating a new order in which what is lost can be illuminated and found anew. She would "light a lamp and sweep out the house and search thoroughly" — these are the three

requirements necessary to bring the work to completion:
(1) To be attentive and alert, (2) to carefully examine all the
threads which go to make up your life, (3) to search tirelessly for the meaning and the message which the loss is
drawing to your attention.

*He said to them, "You read the face of the sky and of
the earth, but you have not recognized the one who is
before you, and you do not know how to read this
moment." (Tm, Log. 91)*

It is an illusion to believe that we have recognized the
nature of things when we have caught them in the pattern
of our thoughts. We are capable of explaining them, putting them in order and doing all sorts of things with them.
Yet we have not recognized "what is before us" and so we
have not participated in the life of the things "of the sky
and of the earth."

It is not wise to persistently follow old customs, nor to
let one's mind dwell on the surface of things. If in a given
moment even the slightest of life's impulses rises from the
depths to awaken your attention, follow its call. Allow
yourself to be surprised by what "is before you." Try to feel
it, let it speak to your being in all its unfamiliarity. Instead
of impressing the moment directly before you into its place
in the chain of past or future, let it work upon you so that
you can examine the riches of its being.

> *Every tree can be recognized by its fruit. People do not*
> *pick figs from thistles, nor gather grapes from briars.*
> *(Luke 6:44)*

Life cares for everything perfectly. Every plant gives the fruit of which it is capable. It would be meaningless if it gave something other than what it gives in perfection.

With human beings it is quite otherwise. What the individual can become is not predestined. One can only say what a person is now. Today they are such and such, but no one can know what they will be tomorrow. Otherwise the ability to decide freely, which is given to humans in the archetypal foundation of their being, would be destroyed. Thanks to this gift, a person can resemble a thistle today and tomorrow can offer figs for harvest.

This is why these words of Jesus admonish us not to judge our fellow humans by the 'type of tree' to which they belong, but by the fruits which they provide for us. To put it another way, we should not judge anyone by their social status or their degree of education. The only things that matter are the joy, the power of their love and the wisdom which they can impart to you.

> *Why do you observe the splinter in your brother's eye*
> *and never notice the great beam in your own? (Luke*
> *6:41)*

We are accustomed to look at the outside of things, to make judgments based on external appearances and to direct our progress according to outward signs or indications. So, from our knowledge of a tiny splinter, we pass judgment on the 'whole' of reality.

The 'great beam' which carries the whole of reality is something we can only find in our own inwardness, in the power of inner attunement, in the inner creative power and in a person's innermost being.

Jesus' words indicate that we should direct our gaze inwards where we can learn to recognize the true core within our colleagues and within the whole of creation. The truth of that which lives and weaves around us is not to be found 'outside' but in our own inwardness.

Let there be among you a man of understanding. When the fruit was ripe, he came quickly with his sickle in his hand and gathered it. Whoever has ears to hear, let him hear. (Tm, Log. 21)

Humanity, as it is today, represents the fruit of several thousand years of evolution. Little by little, from life to life, all the dimensions and planes of our being have developed. We have become capable of acting, willing, feeling, remembering... and just as a fruit becomes ripe, now humanity has ripened to the point that it is ready to leave the former plane of its evolution and leap onto a new plane of becoming.

Jesus' words address the rational person who has arisen within us. This person does not understand the divine perfection of the fruit and is not in a position to perceive it. Reason denies it and ignores it. But this denial and ignorance are in fact the right thing at the right time. They put 'in one's hand the sickle' which can 'gather' the fruit. Without any need for outside intervention, we have cut ourselves off from the path of return which would merely lead us back into a repetition of what we already were.

If the householder knew at what time the thief would come, he would not let anyone break into his house. (Luke 12:39)

The stream of life is so composed that there are within it two polarized skeins which play and interlace with one another, although they arise from two different sources. One skein is symbolized by the householder, the other by the thief.

The householder stands for the outward 'I' of the human being — what today we call the Ego — which normally rules over the decisions and relationships of our life. The thief stands for the power and wisdom of the inner Self who, because of its connection with the universal Wholeness, knows the secrets of life's personal paths of which the householder has no inkling.

The words of Jesus require us to heed the impulses of the inner Self, which like a burglar can surface in an unexpected moment and turn the tables on the Ego's watchfulness so as to get itself a hearing.

The disciples said to Jesus, "Tell us how our end will be." Jesus said, "Have you then discovered the beginning, that you ask about the end? For where the beginning is, there the end will be. Blessed is he who will take his place in the beginning; he will know the end and not taste death." (Tm, Log.18)

Humanity is so bound to the material plane that it is not capable of seeing that life does not run in one stream only, but in two which flow in opposite directions simultaneously. It is true that the stream of linear time proceeds from birth to the moment of death — from a beginning to an end. However, in these words Jesus questions the idea of the 'one-way street' which is stamped on our corporeal life.

He indicates that simultaneously with the stream which takes us from the beginning to the end, there is a current running opposite which is composed of moments of experience which we have taken up in the course of life and worked on in soul and spirit. This inner current leads us from experience to experience, and with each we travel a little further towards its source in the direction of personal enlightenment. Through this process, the line which runs from beginning to end is bent into a circle, so that "he who will take his place in the beginning... will know the end and (will) not taste death."

His disciples said, "When will You become revealed to us and when shall we see You?" Jesus said, "When you lay aside your shame and take off your clothes and like little children put them under your feet and trample them, then will you see the Son of the Living One, and you will not be afraid." (Tm, Log. 37)

Over the last few thousand years our evolution has been accelerating towards increased materialization. We have put on ever thicker clothing so that we perceive ever less of the divine in us and around us. Out of this comes the worried question, "When shall we see You (again)?" Jesus' words do not devalue the material, nor do they condemn the earthly clothing. They only show that the key to liberation from the excessive influence of material things lies in choosing the correct proportion between the spiritual and the earthly aspects of our humanness. First, we should give up being ashamed of our spiritual nature, and despite the dominance of the material and concrete in our culture, concede that we are originally spiritual beings. Then we will become "like little children," which means that we approach nearer to our original source and can understand our material clothing for what it is: a wonderful chance to hold ourselves anchored in the life systems of earth, and with their help collect the necessary life experiences. Putting the clothing underfoot and trampling it is to be understood symbolically as a way of grounding ourselves, in contrast to allowing ourselves to be ruled by matter.

No one puts a piece of new cloth onto an old dress, because the new material pulls away and the tear gets worse. Nor do people put new wine into old wineskins; otherwise, the skins burst, the wine runs out, and the skins are unusable. (Mat 9:16)

The concept of readiness is of fundamental significance in the life of the human being. At every moment we are ready for something. There are no unready humans. We act wisely if we follow that for which, at that particular time in life, we have achieved an inward readiness. In this way we prepare ourselves for a new stage of readiness. We will reach it after we have finished the tasks of the previous plane.

We lose too much of our power and our attunement if we go after things for which we are not ready. It is wiser to put them on one side for later and devote ourselves fully to that which corresponds to our degree of readiness in the moment. With these words Jesus is saying that it is profitless to reach out for things which we desire but for which we lack the foundation to really enjoy. "The new material pulls away from the dress and the tear gets worse." The damage to our development will be greater than the hoped-for gain.

The foxes have their holes and the birds have their nests, but the Son of Man has no place to lay his head and rest. (Tm, Log. 86)

A perfect order, established according to its archetypal pattern, reigned on the planet before humanity was incorporated into the evolution of earth. Every sort of being occupied its own place within the Wholeness: "The foxes have their holes and the birds have their nests."

Humanity brought into this world order something new, unexpected and also destructive. To us was granted the capacity 'to think with our own head'. We humans are not automatically supposed to be part of the common consciousness of all the beings which surround us. Rather, we can form independent thoughts and are therefore in a position to decide freely and so change the usual pattern of our dealings with life. This is expressed in the words, "The Son of Man has no place to lay his head and rest."

We bring with us that for which Earth has not previously prepared a place. Yet we can make our own place when we learn to recognize the archetypal pattern of Earth and bring ourselves into harmony with it.

Why have you come out into the countryside? To see a reed shaken by the wind? (Tm, Log. 78)

The question, why humanity incarnated here among the beings of Earth, is one of the fundamental mysteries of human existence in the here and now. This rhetorical question contradicts the conviction that we evolve as human beings when we persistently make ourselves busy with the chain of cause and effect in the material world surrounding us. The reed shakes for the simple reason that the wind blows.

Too often we forget that we live on earth to exercise ourselves in the fulfillment of our specific role in the universe, and not just to constantly gawk at our surroundings. The fabric of life on earth offers human beings countless chances to broaden their capacity for love, deepen their responsibility for all living things and simultaneously learn how to become a source of creative power and goodness. The words silently point to these areas of our assignment, and we should make them our priority.

He said, "With what can we compare the kingdom of God? It is like a mustard seed. This is the smallest of all the grains of seed which are sown in the earth. Yet once it is sown it comes up and becomes bigger than all the other plants and puts out great branches so that the birds of the air can nest in its shade." (Mark 4:30)

Life shows its face around us in countless manifestations. Not one of these unimaginable numbers of different forms would be constant if it did not possess an inner core. This core is an archetypal pattern where the life qualities of the individual manifestation are inscribed. Figuratively speaking, it is this key alone which establishes that its existence is registered in the book of life. Without this registration it must disappear from the plane of life as quickly as possible.

Human beings also possess such an innermost core through which their place in creation is made visible. It is symbolized by "the smallest of all the grains of seed" which is capable of growing "bigger than all the other plants." This speaks of our capacity to love consciously, and consciously bestow our love on other humans, other beings and other worlds.

It begins with a loving inclination which in itself is scarcely noticeable, but possesses an unimaginable power to stimulate the growth processes of spirit and soul and hasten the development of the All. Figuratively speaking, all "the birds of the air" could nest in the shadow of our love if we were conscious of our power.

If the flesh came into being because of the spirit, it is a wonder. But if spirit came into being because of the body, it is a wonder of wonders.
(Tm, Log. 29)

We humans are not really conscious of our body as a supreme work of Nature's art. It has required an unimaginable concentration of learning experiences to shape the body into a form sufficiently refined that it can receive the human soul as a guest of Earth.

Time is now running out on the long epoch of the soul's adjustment to corporeal circumstances. In future our task will be to effect our body's change into a light body, so that it is also capable of serving as a body beyond the structure of linear space-time. In the words quoted above, this is extolled as the "wonder of wonders."

The first part of the saying relates to the phase of our development which is now ending. In the second part, our attention is directed towards the future, because the fusion of our eternal soul with our earthly self will enable the human being to overcome the division between the spiritual and the corporeal aspects of existence. Then, not only the universe but the earth too will become our permanent home.

The angels and the prophets will come to you and give you those things which are yours. And, on your part, you give them those things which you have, and say to yourselves, 'When will they come and receive what is theirs? (Tm, Log. 88)

In no way does the hierarchical picture of the world corresponds to the nature of the human being. When we content ourselves too humbly with the lowest step, we must recognize above us countless planes together with their beings, by whom we are led, inspired, or simply blessed. This threatens us with the loss of our independence. If we proudly see ourselves as the summit of creation, the danger threatens that we may become so tyrannical that very subtle and even sublime beings must subject themselves to our iron will.

The saying emphasizes the circular nature of the world order. At every step of development — be it ever so high — there is not only giving but receiving too. Only in this way is it possible to maintain the life stream of the universe in its constant circle.

For the human being it is also true that we must not silently accept what is allowed us by other beings who stand higher on the ladder of evolution — here they are described as angels and prophets. We are also capable of giving something which can be offered by no other being in the universe. These are gifts which, on account of our unlimited freedom, are often experienced as unpleasant, even painful. Often they bring with them contrary forces which for the higher beings are a test of their wisdom. This does not imply however that they are meaningless.

Never fear, little flock, your Father has revealed his will to give you a share in the kingdom of God. (Luke 12:32)

One of the most poisonous obstacles on the path of human development is the notion that humans are sinful beings. With a single, simple stroke, these words of Jesus wipe the slate clean of all self-doubt and all reasons for any fears of that sort. At the same time the saying clearly demonstrates the special significance which the human being has for the whole of creation.

The path of human development is doubtless difficult and full of painful setbacks, but our goal is indisputable: the crown of completion awaits us.

If you are bringing your offering to the altar and there remember that your brother has something against you, let your offering lie there before the altar, go and be reconciled with your brother first, and then come back and present your offering. (Mat 5:23)

The concept of God is a human invention, an attempt to name and snare in words what has no name and is so overwhelming that it withdraws itself from direct perception.

However, what is created by the human being can claim no precedence over the human being. Among the beings and presences of the universe, humans are also an embodiment of that which has no name and knows no limits. Only after the Infinite has made itself concrete in a human being — in all the planes and spheres of which it consists — does it receive a personal name and an individual form. Then it can be perceived by every member of the great family of life.

If that which deserves reverence is present more directly in a human being than in the systems of Gods and Goddesses which have been created for the sake of our support, then it is natural that the living relationship with a living human being should have precedence.

Blessed is the lion which the man eats and the lion becomes man; and abominable is the man whom the lion devours, and the man becomes lion. (Tm, Log. 7)

(Translator's note. In the above quotation, I have preferred the German version to the English source cited in the Bibliography. In the English version, the sentence ends "and the lion becomes man.", thus repeating the first line and making a nonsense of the whole text.)

We should not put our faith in everything which happens around us. Human beings are very busy making use of their capacities and powers in a thousand different ways without giving honor to their original source. Such works appear to be great and wonderful, but in truth they are only intended to fascinate human colleagues. Such people hope — mostly unconsciously — to find thereby leverage points which will allow them to establish their power over others. It is meaningless to help others if their real wish is to give validity to what they are not, to their colleagues' cost.

With the phase "abominable is the man," the saying warns us against a lack of awareness in lending our support to others' false powers and claims to power. In contrast, the words, "Blessed is the lion," extols a critical attitude towards such distortions on the part of one's colleagues. Through it, they will learn to distinguish their estranged self-image and their hunger for power from that which is the true expression of their Self.

Recognize what is before your face, and that which is hidden from you will become plain to you. For there is nothing hidden which will not become manifest. (Tm, Log. 5)

Human beings harbor too many feelings of fear, both for themselves and for that which is 'hidden' in them. They do not trust themselves to take a close look at themselves because they are afraid of discovering something unpleasant. They persistently run away from themselves.

When someone flees from his own true face, he is inclined to create a self-willed image of himself and then maintain it artificially. Yet it is impossible to escape one's true own being because the world around us is constantly holding up a mirror to us. All flight is therefore senseless. Sooner or later we must take a critical look at ourselves. Such an examination will only become more difficult as time passes, because the illusory picture which we have devised of ourselves becomes ever more firmly part of us.

But do not fear, every human being is a wonderful world in itself, a cosmos in miniature, perfect and faultless. Love this creation and enjoy what you have and what was given you. Then that which is hidden will reveal itself to you.

Jesus said, "The Kingdom is like a man who had in his field a treasure of which he knew nothing. And after he died, he left it to his son. The son too knew nothing of it. He took the field and sold it. And the one who bought it came and found the treasure while plowing. He began to lend money at interest to whomever he wished. (Tm, Log. 109)

The human being bears within him treasures of which he remains ignorant as long as he does not begin to awaken spiritually. The parable warns us against simply living our life away. It has been given us in order that we may learn little by little to recognize the treasures which we carry within us and raise them to the light, for our own good and the good of others. If our life just drags on from day to day, and we waste it on everyday cares and problems, the danger arises that our sub-conscious 'treasure chamber' will be burgled. Powers could enter which are greedy for our life forces and the spiritual information which we carry. They will begin to misuse our inner capital for their own purposes.

In everyday life such powers manifest themselves in the shape of colleagues who are only concerned to augment their own spiritual, political or economic power. Consciously or unconsciously they seek for forgotten 'treasure chambers' which are worth breaking into. This sort of spiritual pollution of the planet can grow extravagantly because of our human ignorance of 'the treasure hidden in our own field.'

Jesus said, "The Kingdom of the Father is like a woman who is carrying a jar full of flour. While she was walking along a path, still some distance from home, the handle of the jar broke. The flour flowed out behind her on the path. She did not notice it; she had perceived no such disaster. When she reached her house, she set the jar down and found it empty. (Tm, Log. 97)

We are born into a world of abundance, although we do not perceive that it possesses this quality. The Earth Mother gives and gives and gives in limitless loving-kindness. It is on this account that the parable says that the woman "perceived no disaster" until the jar was completely emptied.

Unfortunately we humans do not perceive how limitlessly Earth is overtaxing herself. We bathe in her gifts as if they were the most natural thing in the world. And indeed they are natural, provided we humans are ready on our part to fulfill the tasks for which Earth originally invited us to feast at her table; that means, provided we are ready to walk on the path of self-knowledge and learn to let the abundance which we receive flow onward, so that a cycle arises in which creation can be maintained in its wholeness, without running any danger that one day it will be emptied.

What is your opinion? A man had two sons. He went to the first and said, "My son, go and work in the vineyard today." He answered, "Certainly sir," but did not go. He then turned to the second son and said the same thing to him. This one answered. "I will not go," but afterwards thought better of it and went. Which of the two has fulfilled the father's will? (Mat 21:28)

Neither is wrong! The right to decide freely is an exceptional gift granted to humans. It has value even when it apparently turns against its own source.

The first son symbolizes the beginning stage of the liberation process, which appears to carry a negative sign. This however is necessary, because people can only thoroughly plumb the unexplored depths of their own freedom when they begin inwardly to rebel against the demands which

Church and society have put upon them, expecting them to submit themselves. Although this inner refusal works destructively, there is no reason to see in it anything sinful or something which should occasion guilt feelings.

The second son stands for a more highly developed step of self-liberation, for he consciously resists the automatic reaction to follow the usual ways of doing things or the usual religious ideas. In so doing he creates a free space within himself from which he can decide for himself independently. What he does, he does not do because he must, nor from spite, but from love freely felt.

The kingdom of Heaven is like a treasure which was buried in a field. A man discovered it but buried it again. And in his joy he sold everything he owned and bought the field. (Mat 13:44)

Life is a richly structured stream. It offers opportunities to unfold to all the beings of the universe, corresponding to their evolutionary stage and their role within the Wholeness.

It is worth learning to recognize what parts of this wealth within the living stream, flowing to us so richly and unceasingly, are suited to take us further on our path. If we only choose what serves to maintain the plane which we already reached some time ago, then we will certainly experience life, but not its happy fullness.

The parable teaches us that it is wise not to refuse the opportunities which life offers to leave the beaten track. As soon as we perceive an inspiration of this sort, which is frequently recognizable by a certain excitement, we should at once leave everything which we have already achieved and direct our steps toward the place where we feel "the treasure lies buried in our own field." For this reason it is said, he "goes off in his joy, sells everything he owns and buys the field."

You have heard how it was said to our ancestors, "You shall not kill." But I say to you, anyone who is merely angry with their brother shall be brought before the court. (Mat 5:21)

The decision over life and death is not within human power. Even when it appears otherwise, as when one gives life to another through birth, or takes life by murder, this can only happen when the deed is in accordance with the archetypal pattern of the relevant person's life.

There is however a plane on which people can make decisions on life and death. This is the plane of the Word. It is the plane on which the creative or destructive powers of consciousness take effect. It is through the Word that a person can decisively hinder another on their path, or on the other hand, encourage their development.

By an evil word, yes, even by the silent spread of destructive thoughts, a person's capacity for inner growth can become cramped. Figuratively speaking, their blood is frozen. This happens through subtle effects on planes of power of which people are usually unconscious. Jesus tries to make clear to people through this saying how cautiously they must deal with the powers of their own thoughts and words.

*The kingdom of Heaven is like yeast which a woman
took and mixed in with a great tub of flour till the
whole tub was leavened. (Mat 13:33)*

The moment when unexpected change occurs is one to
which people frequently react with anger and revulsion, but
it is an important element in one's personal development.
It produces a qualitative leap in the linear course of one's
path through life. Consciously or unconsciously, one's quiet
sense of a static, unanalytical acceptance of life becomes
suddenly centered on the question. "Who am I? What is
the meaning of my life?"

It is wise to be alert in handling everything which life
brings. Every time one finds oneself in undesirable circumstances, one should examine whether these, like the yeast,
have not given one's life an unexpected push which can
mean portentous changes. Often the shift is no more than
a hair's breadth, and yet life is never the same thereafter.

*Jesus said, "He who drinks from My mouth will
become like me, and I myself will become he, and the
things that are hidden will reveal themselves to him."
(Tm, Log. 108)*

Listening to words uttered from the mouth is a way of
accepting truth, but is conditioned by our capacity for
mental understanding.

This Logion brings to our attention another possible
way of 'listening'. In this, a person accepts into him or herself the spiritual-emotional quality of the words which are
spoken and allows them to work within as inspiration. In
this case, we do not amass knowledge in linear form, but
allow ourselves to be nursed by the truth itself, that is, to be

changed from within by the truth which we experience. In this way we become that which, through emotional inspiration, we have accepted into ourselves. Of such people, Jesus says that they "will become like me."

In truth I tell you, if anyone says to this mountain, "Raise yourself up and throw yourself into the sea!" and if he doubts not in his heart but believes that what he says will happen, then it will happen. (Mark 11:23)

Doubt and faith are the two poles between which persons continue to oscillate until they have found their center.

In the beginning phase of our evolution both are important. The unpleasant experiences of doubt teach us to recognize the depths of our independence. The comforting experience of faith lets us feel what it means to share in the divine Wholeness.

In a later phase of evolution we experience that doubt has lost its usefulness and now only blocks the path of our growth. As soon as we have recognized this, we should renounce doubt and learn to believe with our whole heart, giving no consideration to whatever difficult situation we are in at the moment, nor how impossible a solution seems. Whoever falls away into doubt at this point impedes their further evolution in quite a momentous way. On the other hand, whoever believes without reservation in the perfection of life — and does not only hope or try to believe it rationally — can really 'uproot mountains', as the words of Jesus say.

Again, the kingdom of Heaven is like a merchant who was looking for fine pearls. When he found an especially valuable pearl, he sold all that he owned and bought it. (Mat 13:45)

Are we in any way aware how many moments are contained in each part of our life? Each moment — like a jewel — is worthy of our attention; it is penetrated with a beauty which belongs to itself alone, and it knows its purpose. This almost wasteful unfolding of the powers of life is founded on a perfect arrangement on planes into which we humans need have no insight. Other powers and beings are taking care of it.

Our attention is demanded elsewhere, and it is elsewhere that we are desired to be alert. To find the "especially valuable pearl," we should choose consciously among life's moments and, drawing on our freedom, decide which opportunities we should leave by the wayside, and which should have priority.

Do not go to meet challenges of this sort with a sour temper, as if someone had awakened you from a deep sleep. Learn to be the co-creator of your fate. Be cautious but not timid. Take decisions with enthusiasm but not heedlessly. Do not be afraid of the inspiration which you feel in yourself. When necessary, take the step which is unforeseen. Life will show you whether you took the right decision. If not, sooner or later you will have the opportunity to correct it.

The eye gives the body light. If your eye is healthy,
then your whole body will be bright. But if your eye
is sick, then your whole body will be in darkness.
(Mat 6:22)

"The words speak of me. Who am I? You have sought me
in the glamour of the ancient Godheads. You have had a
presentiment of my presence in the changing of the sea-
sons. Bread and wine have been sacrificed to me. Now you
are sufficiently grown to learn that there is no distinction
between you and me."

It needs the image of the eye to express what can hardly
be expressed. The divine represents that aspect of our being
which enables us to be part of the universal Whole, and
simultaneously know which little piece is oneself within the
all-embracing Wholeness, and what unique role is ours
within its eternity. For this, the eye is the symbol. On the
one hand, the eye makes it possible for us to see everything
around us. On the other hand, the light which streams into
our consciousness through seeing our Being with information about life. "I am the core of your Being which illumi-
nates you from within and simultaneously I am the Being
of everything which surrounds you as light. As Father and
Daughter (Son) we are one."

Bibliography

Grant, Robert M. with Freedman, David Noel: *The Secret Sayings of Jesus according to the Gospel of Thomas*, Fontana Books, London and Glasgow 1960.

Lorber, Jakob: *Das Grosse Evangelium Johannes*. 11 volumes. Verlag Zluhan, Bietigheim-Bissingen, Germany 1987. Condensed version, *The Great Gospel of John*, translated by Violet Ozols and published by Lorber Verlag, Bietigheim, Germany 1984.

The Nag Hammadi Library, Ed. James M. Robinson, Harper & Row, San Francisco, 1981. (Includes the Gospel of Thomas).

The New Jerusalem Bible, Reader's Edition, Doubleday, New York 1985.

The New Testament, translated by Emil Bock, Urachhaus, Stuttgart, 1991.

Pogačnik, Marko: *Healing the Heart of the Earth*, Findhorn Press, Findhorn 1998

———— *Nature Spirits & Elemental Beings*, Findhorn Press, Findhorn 1997.

———— *Die Landschaft der Gottin. Heilungsprojekte in bedrohten Regionen Europas*, Eugen Diederichs Verlag, Munich 1993.

———— *Schule der Geomantie*, Knaur Verlag, Munich 1996.

———— *Geheimnis Venedig. Modell einer vollkommenen Stadt*, Eugen Dietrichs Verlag, Munich 1997.

Thiede, Carsten Peter and d'Ancona, Matthew: *The Jesus Papyrus*, Weidenfeld and Nicholson, London 1996; also published as *Eyewitness to Jesus*, Doubleday, New York 1996.

Steiner, Rudolf: *The Fifth Gospel*. Rudolf Steiner Press, London 1968.

List of the Sayings of Jesus Quoted in the Book
(in the order of their appearance in the text)

Postscript—22 Years On...

Since I wrote this book that you hold in your hands, 22 years have passed. For me, this relatively long timespan evolved under the sign of the book's last chapter, dedicated to early insights into the Earth's astonishing transformation process. I would like to highlight a few aspects of the continuing story with this short update.

Meeting Pan

At the threshold of the new millennium, on 27 May 2000, I was teaching holistic perception to a group of students in Saarland, Germany. I stood aside of the group in order not to bother it with my presence, when a tall figure appeared before me, emerging from the surrounding forest. I intuitively identified it as the figure of Pan, the classical Greek God of Nature. When he raised his mighty hands, I could clearly see wounds on them, as well as on his feet and his right side. These are known as signs of the 'stigmata'— originating in the crucifixion of Jesus of Nazareth. The next moment, silver rays shot out of Pan's stigmata, touching the corresponding points on my own body. I felt clearly that they had not touched me for personal reasons, but as a representative of the human race.

During the following years, I often thought about the causal background of this astonishing vision in which Pan, representing the world of Nature, identified itself with the Christ—I mean the Christ as I tried to portray him through the different facets of the 'Fifth Gospel'. Yet from the first moment on, it was obvious to me that the stigmata were shown by Pan as a symbol of Christ's presence, and not as a reference to the crucifixion story. Does this mean that, in the meantime, the message and the presence of that cosmic

Pan, as he appeared to me in Saarland

being that Western tradition calls 'the Christ' has incarnated
within the world of nature and its beings, visible and
invisible?

My interpretation is as follows: Whilst the human race
has struggled for two millennia with the meaning of
Christ's message—either transforming it into various,
more-or-less rigid religious institutions, or denying it
totally as something insignificant for humanity's future—
his impulse has travelled through the different layers and
dimensions of the Earth. Through this process the Earth,
the planet of Gaia, has been changed fundamentally. The
Earth regained the light structure and its multi-
dimensionality that was lost during the billions of years of
its passage through the secret of matter. As a con-

sequence, the process of Earth transformation—which I report in the last chapter of the present book—was initiated and moved forward.

Pan appeared in the Saarland forest in order to make clear that the journey of the Christ impulse through the inner Earth is complete. The Christ impulse appears once again to humanity—not descending from the heavens, but revealing itself through the elemental worlds of nature and the wisdom of Gaia, the Earth.

In this context, I interpret the silvery rays that fell upon my stigmata points as an invitation issued to the human race to open itself to the presence and message of the Christ, transcending all ideological and religious structures and patterns. Let us listen, from this moment on, to the voice of Nature and the Earth as an embodiment of cosmic consciousness, power and love, that the Western tradition refers to as 'the Christ'. Human beings are called upon to open themselves to the transmuted Earth and to Nature as the relevant source of this new consciousness, as revealed through the Fifth Gospel—which is my attempt to show its hidden presence within the Gospels of John, Luke, Matthew, Mark and Thomas.

The holistic perception of reality

Since I met Pan and understood his intention to inspire us to experience the Christ consciousness through the elemental world of Nature, I have intensified my efforts to develop ways of holistic perception of Nature and its beings. Human beings should be able to overcome the superficial perception of the five senses and to connect with the deeper layers of Gaia's Earth. It is there that we can find peace and security, but also the knowledge of how to travel safely within the ongoing Earth Changes.

My method of perception was initially inspired by the

saying of Christ, as reported by the Gospel of St Luke: 'But understand this: If the owner of the house had known at what hour the thief was coming, he would not have let his house be broken into. You also must be ready, because the Son of Man will come at an hour when you do not expect him.' (Luke 12: 39–40)

The key word that helps translate the meaning of this saying into the instruction concerning the multi-dimensional perception is the expression 'The Son of Man'. My translation of this phrase into modern language would be: 'the son of the human being'—alias a new generation of human beings that embodies the qualities addressed by the Christ two millennia ago, at the threshold of our era.

My intuition says that 'the householder' stands for the rational aspect of consciousness that has taken dominance over all aspects of human culture, science and civilization. Rationality controls the process of perception of the modern human being up to the smallest detail, making sure that 'the thief' cannot enter human experience. The thief in this case stands for intuitions, impulses of the heart and visions that presently are under the total control of modern rationality.

In a practical sense, such control functions in such a way that the rational mind overcomes the perception process, before it is even able to develop. As result, it declares all possible perceptions of living and loving reality as non-existent. Human consciousness is thus falsely assured that nothing exists beyond the horizon of intellectual discourse. Christ's words emphasize that to be able to perceive reality in its wholeness, one should take on the role of the burglar and find a tiny crack to break in to one's own house, that is currently controlled by one's own mind.

To overcome this situation, my advice is that one should teach the rational mind to step aside for a moment and allow one's intuition to read the message first. Only a split second is needed for complex information to be received in its entirety. Only in the next stage of the process is the mind enabled to decode the perceived message and to translate it into a logical statement. This means that it is not necessity to suppress the logical mind. Rather, it should be moved from the initial to the final place in the process of perception. Jesus's relevant saying in relation to this is the well-known statement: 'The last shall be first and the first last.'

To be able to gain insights into true reality, the rational mind's right to control human perception should clearly be denied. On the other hand, we should persist with the human being's right to perceive reality, in its multi-dimensional wholeness. Otherwise, no insights could be gained into the real state of the Earth's process of trans-formation, and as a consequence human beings would be lost in a process of not knowing. We would have no idea how crucial it is for humanity's future to take part in the Earth's process of transformation now—and finding one's place within it *as a co-creator*.

An example of holistic perception

To give an example as to how one can teach oneself to overcome the control of the mind, I propose *perception through the back of the body*. Since our perception is mainly controlled through our eyes, our sensitivity and intuition get much more freedom to perceive true reality in a holistic way if the object being perceived—for example a tree, stone or landscape—is perceived through one's back.

Start by simply turning your back to the phenomenon you would like to explore, in all its multi-dimensional entirety. Be aware of the first, even tiny, vibration or per-haps movement of your body that you feel. In that very moment, allow your consciousness to find an emotion, a colour or an image that is in resonance with the quality that you have sensed. All this should happen in the same instant that you open your back and receive the tiny impulse. Then take time for yourself—still turning your back to the phenomena—to ponder over the experience, and to let the rational mind enter slowly into the process, so that you can become conscious of what you have perceived.

Perception through the back can be enhanced if you position your feet so that the back chakras of perception are more open. Your heels should be apart as much as possible, whilst the big toes touch each other.

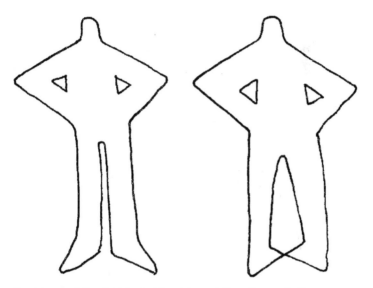

Positions of the feet to support perception through the body's back

Another possibility is that you approach the chosen phenomenon—be it a tree, a stone or a cultural monument—backwards. Take a few steps backwards, then stop for some moments and dive into the process of perception as described above. Then take a few more steps backward, stop again and try to discern the difference in perception. Since phenomena have an energy field composed of different layers—experiencing diverse layers will teach you to discern different aspects of reality.

Be aware of following preconditions for holistic perception:

— Holistic perception means that you have decided to abandon subjective-objective distance. Holistic perception can only come into being through the observer feeling at one with the observed.

— Do not aim for objective results. The multidimensional reality is as much objective as it is subjective. Seeing and understanding it this way, the reality of life can be filled again with love and light.

— Become co-creator of your own, and Gaia's, reality. Do not fear interaction in the process of perception. On the contrary, the holistic perceptions can come into being only if you creatively cooperate with the process through which perception of reality comes into being.

— Even more, in the conditions of the renewed Earth body, holistic perception is a guarantee that the reality of life continues to exist.

'Holographic Touch' exercises

Another stream of development that started after I finished this book has to do with discovering creative tools through which it is possible to stimulate personal development. This is done in such a way that the practitioner is able to tune in to the new emerging reality and to prepare her or his body and consciousness for the coming changes.

After the year 1997, when the Earth changing process arrived to the threshold of my awareness, I started to perceive and formulate body exercises that in the beginning I called 'Holographic Touch'. I use the phrase 'touch' because I envision these exercises as a gentle push to bring into movement some processes of change within the human psyche, consciousness and body, as well within the world we inhabit. Later I started to call them 'Gaia Touch, Body Exercises and Rituals'. They are dedicated to deepening the relationship between human beings and the earthly universe.

These exercises were inspired by elementary and other beings from different sacred places of the Earth where, together with groups of interested people, I performed healing and regenerating works. Beings of Gaia offered, so to say, these exercises to their fellow beings in order to help us attune better to the newly-emerging multidimensional nature of our home planet and its subtle inhabitants. The exercises represent a combination of body movements and 'imaginations', a kind of body cosmogram.

The authentic power of the Gaia Touch cosmograms is generated through the interaction between the exercising person and the beings of those sacred places that inspired the cosmograms. Exercises also work in the opposite direction. By performing a Gaia Touch exercise, one supports the given place and its beings in their striving to protect the true identity of their place and to strengthen its contribution to the changing Earth.

A Gaia Touch personal ritual, created to change foreign patterns projected upon the Christ's presence, started to appear in Bosnia when visiting the Bogomil necropolis at Radimlja, near Stolac. Standing beside a 'Stećak'—a kind of Bogomil stone house carved for the deceased—my hands were lifted to form a cross and then folded inwardly. At the same time I heard a voice saying, 'the Christ is within you'. Bogomils, as a medieval religious movement parallel to the French Cathars, denied the right of the Christian Church to represent Christ in the form of an institution or outward 'church'. They summoned people to find the integral divinity within them, at the core of their own heart.

A few years later, I was preparing a workshop to interact

with the cityscape of Rio de Janeiro. Standing in front of the
famous gigantic sculpture of Christ extending its arms over
Rio, I decided to perform the above-mentioned Bogomil
exercise. But I immediately received a denying gesture from
Christ's presence, which led me to realize that the Christ in
Rio is not hanging upon a cross but extends his arms to bless
the world and its beings. Further, the Christ of Rio wanted
me to be aware that it is not by chance that he is standing
upon a granite rock called Corcovado. As with other famous
rocks of Rio de Janeiro, Corcovado is being raised out of the
Earth at the rate of two millimeters per year.

As reported at the beginning of this Postscript, Pan made
me aware that the Christ power and wisdom are rising out
of the core of the Earth during the present 'Second Coming'. The Rio Christ made me similarly aware by demanding
that the exercise start with him rising out of the Earth,
together with the Corcovado rock. Also, I was urged to
include in the Gaia Touch exercise the gesture of transformation of all the false patterns projected upon the
Christ's presence during the last two millennia.

Here is the final form of the Christ ritual as part of the
Gaia Touch body exercises:

*Gaia Touch personal ritual to connect with the Christ
within*
   — Position your hands diagonally into the space behind
      your back in order to indicate that the new gen-
      eration of Divinity, represented by the Christ,
      approaches the world through the core of Gaia.
   — Stretch out your arms on both sides, so that your body
      makes the form of a cross, as if you would embrace
      the whole world.
   — After a while bend your elbows, so that your palms
      come to rest on your chest, being aware that Divinity
      is not only vibrating in the width of the universe, but
      is present also at the centre of your heart space.

Gaia Touch ritual to connect with the Christ within

— Then move your arms towards the original cross-like position, but this time start the gesture with the back sides of your hands touching each other. This is a gesture of pushing away all the false patterns projected upon the face of the Christ.
— While your hands are now in the cross-like position again, turn the palms towards the world in front of you and radiate from your palms' centre, powers of

transmutation in order to change the false patterns. Use the colour violet for this purpose.

— Then, position again your hands into the space behind your back. Pause for a moment, during which time you should transfer your attention to your feet, imagining that the chakras of your feet glow with light.

— Now you can start the ritual from the beginning. Repeat it a few times and then listen to its echo within yourself.

Marko Pogačnik
Šempas, Slovenia, 1 July 2019

Books to challenge  *your perception of reality*

A message from Clairview

We are an independent publishing company with a focus on cutting-edge, non-fiction books. Our innovative list covers current affairs and politics, health, the arts, history, science and spirituality. But regardless of subject, our books have a common link: they all question conventional thinking, dogmas and received wisdom.

Despite being a small company, our list features some big names, such as Booker Prize winner Ben Okri, literary giant Gore Vidal, world leader Mikhail Gorbachev, modern artist Joseph Beuys and natural childbirth pioneer Michel Odent.

So, check out our full catalogue online at
www.clairviewbooks.com
and join our emailing list for news on new titles.

office@clairviewbooks.com

CLAIRVIEW